LAWFARE

Studies in Critical Social Sciences Book Series

Haymarket Books is proud to be working with Brill Academic Publishers (www.brill.nl) to republish the *Studies in Critical Social Sciences* book series in paperback editions. This peer-reviewed book series offers insights into our current reality by exploring the content and consequences of power relationships under capitalism, and by considering the spaces of opposition and resistance to these changes that have been defining our new age. Our full catalog of *SCSS* volumes can be viewed at https://www.haymarketbooks .org/series_collections/4-studies-in-critical-social-sciences.

LAWFARE

The Criminalization of Democratic
Politics in the Global South

EUGENIO RAÚL ZAFFARONI,
CRISTINA CAAMAÑO
AND VALERIA VEGH WEIS

TRANSLATED BY
FEDERICO BAREA AND CASEY GOUGH

Haymarket Books
Chicago, IL

First published in 2023 by Brill Academic Publishers, The Netherlands
© 2023 Koninklijke Brill NV, Leiden, The Netherlands

Published in paperback in 2024 by
Haymarket Books
P.O. Box 180165
Chicago, IL 60618
773-583-7884
www.haymarketbooks.org

ISBN: 979-8-88890-228-8

Distributed to the trade in the US through Consortium Book Sales and
Distribution (www.cbsd.com) and internationally through Ingram Publisher
Services International (www.ingramcontent.com).

This book was published with the generous support of Lannan Foundation,
Wallace Action Fund, and the Marguerite Casey Foundation.

Special discounts are available for bulk purchases by organizations and
institutions. Please call 773-583-7884 or email info@haymarketbooks.org for more
information.

Cover design by Jamie Kerry and Ragina Johnson.

Printed in the United States.

Library of Congress Cataloging-in-Publication data is available.

Contents

Foreword to the Spanish Edition

The authors, three renowned professors of the Law School of the University of Buenos Aires, analyze in depth a phenomenon that, though found worldwide, has developed systematically and with an undesirable frequency in Latin America: the use of the judiciary, especially in the application of criminal law, to interfere in politics.[1] This is *lawfare*, a legal war with illegitimate ends, as my lawyers put it in 2016. As part of a decades-long fight against social policies designed to eradicate poverty and diminish deep social inequalities, the elites of our region, together with the defenders of the interests of international financial capital, have promoted corruption to the category of a "cosmic evil," pointing to it as the origin and cause of all social problems. Of course, no one approves of corrupt rulers. But this sort of fight against corruption is merely a pretext used by those sectors to attack governments legitimately elected by popular vote.

The courts have become the sphere in which those defeated at the polls seek to impose their own interests over popular sovereignty. In this way, some sectors of the judiciary and of the different organs of the justice system, with the opportunistic support of the hegemonic media, have attacked popular governments concerned with the defense of national interests. Their objective is to criminalize and destroy politics, trying to instill in the collective conscience the idea that all politicians are corrupt. The physical destruction of the adversary is no longer adequate; what is desired is his legal and political death.

Under the pretext of fighting corruption, they violate the legal principle of due process and the constitutional guarantees of the accused. As the authors of this book point out, every case that has occurred in the different countries of our region follows the same method: a part of the press, politically involved, fabricates a fact and widely disseminates it (a lie told a thousand times eventually becomes a "truth"); relying exclusively on this fictional news, the judicial police opens an investigation; the public prosecutor's office goes in search of elements that can formally support the accusation; even when no evidence is found, the accusation is still often filed, as happened in Brazil, with the assertion that "I have no proof, but I am convinced." Then it is only necessary to "identify some judges willing to collaborate," either because they see their long-awaited chance for fame, or a more concrete, personal advantage. Every

---

1   Former president of the Federative Republic of Brazil between January 1, 2003 and December 31, 2010.

news cycle exposes the intimate and private life of the defendants on the basis of these so-called *vazamentos* (information leaks), a term which camouflages the operation of shrewdly selecting one or more facts and transmitting them with full intention to "colleagues" in the media, especially on television. Faced with the impossibility of proving something that did not happen, the accusers resort to illegal wiretapping, compulsory subpoenas, and preventive imprisonment of both the accused and their families. Such are the mechanisms used to achieve the "confession" of the Informant (this is the name given in Spanish-speaking countries to those who "are capable of inventing any situation to obtain a benefit"), for whom the "reward" is freedom itself and, at least in Brazil, the chance to keep a good part of the proceeds of the crime they confessed to committing. Once the confession has been extracted from the informant then, even without the slightest additional proof, the accused is tried and convicted. If the crime is still not proven, then the bizarre category of an "indeterminate fact" is invoked. The circus is complete when the condemnatory sentence is confirmed by a court that remains partial and committed to the political and economic interests of the ruling classes.

These are the legal means for imprisoning an enemy and preventing him from intervening in political life. The mass media, with television at the forefront, then assume the task of incessantly spreading the judicial decision, thereby granting legitimacy to an absolutely spurious process.

With the enemy removed from the political arena, the way is open for the election of men and women loyal to the interests of the market and indifferent to the needs of the population, especially the poorest. National sovereignty is violated by the sale of large public companies, always sold at prices far below their actual worth, in operations that reveal a total disregard for the environment and for so many other basic rights of the people.

The research carried out by these three authors describes very well what happened in many countries, including Brazil, where they tried to impose political and legal death on me. I was a victim of the machination analyzed here: based on false news published in a newspaper, I was investigated, prosecuted and convicted by the so-called "Operation Car Wash" (*Operação Lava Jato*), which condenses the worst of the Brazilian justice system. Today, no one doubts that there were sectors of the Federal Police and the Federal Public Prosecutor's Office, under the orders of a notoriously biased judge eager for self-promotion, that formed an organization guided by the objective of annulling my political rights in order to prevent me from running again for the presidency of the Republic and to ensure the Workers' Party (*Partido dos trabalhadores,* PT) its fifth consecutive term in office. With a speed never before seen in the conduct of other proceedings, the Federal Regional Court confirmed the sentence, fulfilling the public promise expressly made by its president that the case would be judged before the elections.

They did not take into account my defense. They did not take into account the unconditional support given to me by the social movements, the workers and all those people who, from different parts of the country, held the moving Free Lula Vigil (*Vigília Lula Livre*) in front of the federal police building where I was imprisoned. They did not take into account the reactions of the international political and legal community. And instead of leaving Brazil, as they suggested, I decided to go to jail and, from there, face the cowards who accused me without evidence. It was not in vain, since at least one of the greatest conquests of civilized societies, and one that our Federal Constitution guarantees, was already reestablished by the Federal Supreme Court: the presumption of innocence. A measure that put an end to my unjust imprisonment, which was determined before the higher court ruled on the appeal filed in my defense.

Today I am free, but I am not free. My political rights are still curtailed, even before the appeal I lodged with the higher court has been judged.

My congratulations to Professors Cristina Caamaño, Valeria Vegh Weis, and Raúl Zaffaroni, who, with academic rigor, have shown how "true criminal law" has been distorted and given rise to "shameful criminal law," which serves to transform the judiciary into an instrument of political persecution of all those here in our beloved Latin America who raise their voices and arms in defense of the abandoned, who stand firm in the face of the powerful representatives of international financial capital and the rulers servile to the market god. I ardently hope that the authors' objective is achieved: "to take the study of law out of the ivory tower" and place it "at the service of the people."

Inácio Lula da Silva
President of Brazil (2022–2026)

Prologue

It seems that all the geniuses in the history of the world created their brilliant works in times of plague, and so we could hardly do less! If Isaac Newton discovered gravity, then at least during the pandemic we might, in our distant corner of the world, have our own small revelation: to bring the stratospheric language of the judiciary down, by sheer force of gravity, to a level all of us can understand.

Yes, ladies and gentlemen, our contribution would be to decode the encrypted record of the courts that is causing so much confusion. And it was enough to turn on the television to realize that what has really been quarantined is criminal law! Truth be told, criminal law has been beaten to a pulp and then some. When one of the incumbents falters (i.e., democratic elections are not won, the opposition is too strong, or a distracting measure is needed to sweep the reserves) criminal law assumes a role it has no right to play.

This concerned us because we three authors have studied and taught passionately at the Law School of the University of Buenos Aires (and yes, it is politically correct to use "passionate" to describe the unpaid, or almost unpaid, work of public university teaching). The three of us have learned and taught that the state exercises violence, and that the best thing to do is to keep it contained so that we do not all become its victims. We have also learned and taught that state violence, in times of democracy, is exercised by the police in the form of punitivity, and that if we want to stop it, the best tool is constitutional guarantees. What are these guarantees? That I will not be imprisoned without a conviction, that I will be allowed to exercise my right to defend myself against the accusations levied against me, that the judge who resolves the case will not be angry with me, and many others. Yes, the three authors have learned and taught that constitutional guarantees are not tantamount to a Bolshevik revolution; they prevent punitivity from getting completely out of control (and imprisoning us all).

The three authors have also enjoyed the incomparable privilege of visiting different offices and buildings within our beloved Argentine judiciary. We know very well the good and the bad of our penal system and how dangerous it can be for judges to use their power to benefit one politician or harm another. Judges have to be there to ensure that constitutional guarantees are complied with, and if they are distracted by also having to conduct investigations, they simply will not be able to handle it all.

The three of us – Raul, Cristina, and Valeria – are worried. Our democracy is too young and courageous to be put at risk by judges who respond to foreign agendas or careerism. We know that only a strong and attentive society can prevent us from being manipulated, and that under grandiloquent accusations of corruption, puppet politicians who open the doors to financial totalitarianism are putting on a show for us. And we are committed to bringing academia – and especially legal academia – out of its supposedly apolitical ivory tower. Law is too deep in the mud to pretend to be neutral. This book is intended to help put academia at the service of the people. It falls to us to do so by clarifying the obscure language in which the judiciary speaks, and by exposing the distortions of the media in an effort to encourage an open and honest conversation about what sort of judiciary and criminal law we really need. Having made this effort, the book really has only one goal: that we pay attention, because history is made by the people.

Acknowledgements

Before beginning the journey, we wish to express our deepest gratitude to the researchers that helped make this book possible (Rodrigo Murad do Prado, Analía Ploskenos, Rodrigo Barcellos de Oliveira Machado, Felipe Fuertes, Florencia Maldonado, Javier García Sierra, Javier Guillardoy, Karen Navarro, Leandro D'Ascenzo, Luciana Casal, Maximiliano Nicolás, Tamara Rotundo, Viviana García Sierra), to the incomparable Lula, and to Eli and Atilio for their contributions to this collective work that we hope will contribute to the unveiling of so much injustice.

Notes on Contributors

Cristina Caamaño
Comptroller of the Argentine Federal Intelligence Agency, member of the INECIP Board of Directors, and Visiting Lecturer at the University of Buenos Aires School of Law. She was a prosecutor for the Correctional and Criminal Court of Appeals, Secretary of the Operational Security for the Department of National Security, Director of the Committee on Criminal Law, Lecturer at the University of the Madres de la Plaza de Mayo, and Lecturer and Member of the Advisory Board for the UBA Higher Education in Federal Prison Program. She is the author of *Manual práctico para defenderse de la cárcel* (Inecip, 2006), *Manual para el preso extranjero* (Inecip, 2009), and *El delito de administración fraudulenta* (Fabian Di, 2013). She was the Argentine expert in *Ejecución de la pena privativa de libertad: una mirada comparada*, published by the Eurosocial Program in 2014.

Eugenio Raúl Zaffaroni
Doctor of Juridical Sciences, Notary, Professor Emeritus of the University of Buenos Aires, Secretary General of the Latin American Association of Criminology and Penal Law, and Vice President of the International Association of Penal Law. He holds honorary degrees from forty-five Latin American and European universities. In 2009 he received the Stockholm Prize in Criminology. He served as a Justice of the Argentine Supreme Court, and as General Director of the United Nations Latin American Institute for the Prevention of Crime and Treatment of Offenders. He is currently serving as a judge on the Inter-American Court of Human Rights. He is the author of *Criminology and Criminal Policy Movements* (University Press of America, 2013), *Manual de Derecho Penal* (Ediar, 2006), *Tratado de Derecho Penal. Parte General* (Ediar, 2004), *Derecho Penal* (Ediar, 2000) and *La Palabra de los Muertos* (Ediar, 2011).

Valera Vegh Weis
Doctor of Juridical Sciences (UBA), Specialist in Penal Law (UBA), and Magistrate in International Public Law (New York University). She is currently a Research Fellow at the Zukunftskolleg at Konstanz University in Germany. She was previously an Alexander von Humboldt Foundation Postdoctoral Fellow (Berlin Freie Universität) and an Associate Researcher at the Max Planck Institute for Legal History and Legal Theory. She is also a Lecturer of Criminology and Transitional Justice at the UBA School of Law and at the National University of Quilmes, and Vicepresident of the Latin American Institute of Criminology

and Social Development. She is the author of *Criminalization of Activism* (Routledge, 2021) and *Marxism and Criminology: A History of Penal Selectivity* (Brill, 2017, and Haymarket Books, 2018), winner of the 2017 Choice Book Award and the 2019 Outstanding Book Award. She was also awarded the Critical Criminologist of the Year Award in 2021.

Introduction to the English Version

Valeria Vegh Weis

The word "lawfare" circulates daily in the media outlets of Latin America. But what does it mean? What are its characteristics? Where does the term come from? Why use an anglicism in the Global South? Is it a new phenomenon? What is the role of the United States and the Global North in lawfare? Is there a link between lawfare and corruption, and if so, how can it be fought? These questions must be answered from a broad and interdisciplinary perspective that brings together different aspects of the phenomenon. From this broad perspective, and in continuity with the Spanish and Portuguese editions, the English version of this book proposes to delve into criminal law, criminal procedure, and criminology, and to introduce the English-speaking public to a comprehensive vision of so-called "lawfare."

The origin of the term can be traced to the turn of the 20th century, when two Chinese colonels, Qiao Liang and Wang Xiangsui, published the book *Unrestricted Warfare.*[1] They argued that war in the traditional sense of the word was not enough to explain new geopolitical configurations. They proposed three more subtle dimensions of warfare that do not require missiles: "psychological warfare" aimed at transforming emotions and influencing the psyche of the population, "media warfare" to control public opinion, and "judicial warfare," used to criminalize dissent.

Almost at the same time, an American Air Force colonel, Charles Dunlap, focused particularly on the legal dimension of war and proposed the neologism "lawfare," a contraction of "law" and "warfare." With this term, Dunlap characterized the 21st-century form of warfare as being intrinsically linked to using law as a weapon of war. In other words, that lawfare is a mode of warfare in which the judicial system is used to accomplish a military objective.[2]

Dunlap argued that lawfare was a product of the "hyper-legalism" used by third-world countries and the international community to discredit U.S. interventions abroad, putting national security at risk. More precisely, the colonel argued that the origin of lawfare began in the international reaction to the

---

1 Liang Qiao y Xiangsui Wang (1999) *Unrestricted Warfare*, Beijing: PLA Literature and Arts.
2 Dunlap, Charles (2001) "Law and Military Interventions: Preserving Humanitarian Values in 21st Conflicts. Working Paper." Humanitarian Challenges in Military Intervention Conference, Carr Center for Human Rights Policy. Kennedy School of Government, Harvard University. Washington DC, Nov. 29, http://people.duke.edu/~pfeaver/dunlap.pdf, p. 2.

bombings in Kosovo and Serbia by NATO in 1999. It was then, Dunlap argued, that the media and the international community began to use legal language, and especially international human rights law, to delegitimize military intervention and the role of the United States. The term "lawfare" was then applied extensively during the administration of U.S. President George W. Bush, and ascribed to "weak actors" who took advantage of international forums, legal processes, and terrorist acts in order to undermine the United States.[3] Dunlap asks whether international law might not be weakening the US military's ability to effectively intervene, increasing the risks posed to civilians, and ultimately becoming part of the problem instead of part of the solution.[4]

In the same vein, Jack Goldsmith argued that "various nations, NGOs, academics, international organizations, and other actors in the international community are weaving a web of international law and institutions that today threaten the interests of the U.S. government."[5] Likewise, Christi Bartman described lawfare as "the manipulation or exploitation of the international legal system to complement military and political objectives."[6] However, years later, Dunlap reassembled his original conceptualization and argued that lawfare is actually a neutral tool and could even be used by the United States as part of its foreign defense.[7] In this sense, Dunlap proposed to define lawfare as "the strategy of using (or even misusing) law as a substitute for traditional military means to achieve an operational objective," and advocated for its use both as a response to "enemy" war campaigns that attempt to delegitimize U.S. war aims and interventions, and as a means of expanding and legitimizing the war aims themselves.[8]

More recently, other authors have continued along these lines by addressing lawfare in both dimensions. From England, Orde Kittrie argues that lawfare has acquired two differentiated forms.[9] On the one hand, "instrumental lawfare" refers to the instrumental use of legal tools to obtain the same or similar effects to those traditionally obtained through traditional military intervention. On the

---

3   Carter, Phillip (2005) "Legal Combat: Are Enemies Waging War in Our Courts," *Slate*, Apr. 4, http://slate.msn.com/id/2116169.

4   Dunlap, op cit 2001, p. 1.

5   Goldsmith, Jack (2020) "The Soleimani Strike: One Person Decides," *Lawfare Blog*, Jan. 3, https://www.lawfareblog.com/soleimani-strike-one-person-decides.

6   Bartman, Christi Scott (2010) *Lawfare: Use of the Definition of Aggressive War by the Soviet and Russian Federation Governments*. NT: Cambridge Scholars Publishing, p. 3–4.

7   Dunlap, Charles (2009) Lawfare: a Decisive Element of 21st-Century Conflicts?, Joint Force Quarterly, n. 54, pp. 34–39, https://scholarship.law.duke.edu/faculty scholarship/3347/.

8   Ansah, Tawia (2010) Lawfare: A Rhetorical Analysis, Case Western Reserve Journal of International Law, v. 43, n. 87, https://scholarlycommons.law.case.edu/jil/vol43/iss1/6.

9   Kittrie, Orde F. (2016) *Lawfare Law as a Weapon of War*, Oxford: OUP.

other hand, there is "disparate lawfare compliance-exploitation," which refers to the use of law to gain advantages in traditional armed conflict, particularly through the law of war. The author argues that, so far, the United States has been largely a victim of lawfare. The reluctance to ratify international treaties and to become a member of the International Criminal Court is due, according to Kittrie, to American fears of the international community, and the consequent use of international law as a weapon of denunciation against it. In this regard, Kittrie recalls that, under the George W. Bush administration, the United States even sought to diminish the role of the International Criminal Court through the so-called "Article 98" agreements signed with more than one hundred countries, which resolved to reject the jurisdiction of the court over American defendants. However, the author also argues that lawfare can consist of creating national laws enabling trials against terrorist groups and their financiers, among other modalities that could benefit US national security policy.

John Comaroff, for his part, adhered to Dunlap's first conception, understanding the term lawfare from a negative perspective, no longer in terms of US interests, but rather as a tool framed within the geopolitical dynamics dominated by imperialism and post-colonialism. From this point of view, Comaroff defined lawfare as "the recourse to legal instruments, to the violence inherent in the law, to commit acts of political coercion."[10] Years later he and Jean Comaroff reanalyzed the term, which they then described as imperialism's use of "its own penal codes, its administrative procedures, its states of emergency, its statutes and injunctions and court orders, to discipline its subjects by means of legible and legal violence."[11] However, the authors note that lawfare can also become "a weapon of the weak, turning authority against itself and demanding resources, recognition, voice, integrity and sovereignty in the courts."[12]

In this direction, Hedi Viterbo summarizes the two opposing visions of the term. On the one hand, as the law of empire, lawfare implies the deployment of law by the most powerful states in the framework of planning, executing and legitimizing their controversial military objectives. In this sense, lawfare can operate as a replacement for traditional warfare or as a support for it. Lawfare in international human rights law, on the other hand, involves attempts by individuals, liberal human rights organizations and other political entities to harness the law to restrict or rebuke violent state policies and practices.

---

10   Comaroff, John L. (2001) "Law, culture, and colonialism: a foreword," *Law and Social Inquiry*, v. 26, n. 2, pp. 101–110.

11   Comaroff, Jean y Comaroff, John (2007) "Law and disorder in the postcolony," *Social Anthropology*, v. 15, n. 2, pp. 133–152, p. 144.

12   Comaroff, Jean y Comaroff, John (2007) op cit, p. 145.

The question, then, is how does this normative[13] concept, created in the Global North, transfer to Latin America, where there are currently no wars or military processes between states? Notwithstanding the absence of wars between countries, it is possible to identify in Latin America dynamics in which the law is used in a warlike manner to justify the subjugation of the rule of law *within* the borders of each state. What is more, just as at the international level, lawfare, at least in one of its conceptions, comes to replace or, subsidiarily, to reinforce the direct use of military force, in Latin America, lawfare seems to replace, whenever the play of forces makes it possible, the role of traditional military coups. Thus, criminal cases brought within the framework of democratic governments under the umbrella of "corruption" serve to delegitimize and remove opposition political leaders from the game without the need to reach a state of lawlessness. In the words of Rafael Bielsa and Pedro Peretti:

> The magistrates have been co-opted in replacement of the military, who were already too discredited in the eyes of the population for their leading role in the violation of Human Rights during the dictatorships. What is new is not the irruption of the judges into the political arena (judiciary and politics are not necessarily mutually exclusive concepts), but rather the brazenness and the prominence acquired by the judicial clique. This is what is new ... The real power no longer needs the [representatives of the military juntas] Jorge Rafael Videla (1925–2013) nor Humberto de Alencar Castelo Branco (1897–1967), that marshal who in 1964 usurped the government in Brazil. Now they are supplanted by judges like Sergio Moro [the judge who indicted Lula da Silva in Brazil].[14]

Moreover, the elements proposed in *Unrestricted Warfare* (1999) seem particularly key when analyzing Latin American realities and the warlike use of law within democratic frameworks. "Psychological warfare" takes shape in the insistence on cracks or dichotomous divisions between simplified political positions (populism vs. anti-populism) or between opposition and officialism (Kirchnerism vs. anti-Kirchnerism in Argentina, PT vs. anti-PT in Brazil). The "media war" acquires exacerbated dimensions due to the problematic concentration of the media. Finally, the "judicial war" highlights the fact that, in this region, it is a non-democratic power that, exempt from civic control, has

---

13   Duve, Thomas (2018) Global Legal History: Setting Europe. in Perspective. In: Pihlajamäki, Heikki; Dubber, Markus D.; Godfrey, Mark (eds.). *The Oxford Handbook of European Legal History*, Oxford: OUP.

14   Op cit, p. 12.

legitimized military dictatorships[15] as well destitution processes,[16] and that has not experienced the post-dictatorial transformation that shaped the executive and legislative powers of our countries, primarily through the mechanisms of civic background control.[17]

Within this framework, some terms defined from the Global South include those of Bielsa and Peretti, who describe lawfare as "the illegitimate use that the judiciary makes of national or international law with the aim of harming an opponent, in the struggle to obtain a certain political objective, such as the exclusion of a candidacy for public office," and add that it is "a distortion in the application of the law executed by judges at the service of the political-economic-media power, which persecutes the opponents of the inequitable appropriation model."[18] Maximiliano Rusconi points out that this is a violation of due process and an application of criminal selectivity to an even greater degree than that present in the ordinary criminal system for the prosecution of governments characterized by a greater social sensitivity.[19] Graciana Peñafort, a lawyer in some prominent cases cataloged as "lawfare," defines the term as "political persecution that uses the law as a tool and that, in addition to the law, requires the media for its installation. In addition to persecution, it has a psychological effect on politics."[20] For their part, from Brazil, Azar and Tavares da Motta define it as "the manipulation of legal institutes and of the judiciary itself to obtain results in the political sphere (and) take the political dispute beyond the ballot box."[21]

Building on these precedents, it is possible to suggest that although forms of individual physical destruction of political dissidents, as in the case of

15 http://www.saij.gob.ar/corte-suprema-justicia-nacion-federal-ciudad-autonoma-bue nos-aires-acordada-sobre-reconocimiento-gobierno-provincial-nacion-fa30996876-1930 -09-10/123456789-678-6990-30ts-eupmocsollaf.

16 Zanin, Cristiano, Martins, Valeska y Valim, Rafael (2019) Lawfare: Uma Introdução. São Paulo: Contracorrente.

17 CELS 2016, op cit.

18 Bielsa, Rafael y Peretti, Pedro (2019) Lawfare. Guerra judicial-mediática. Desde el Primer Centenario hasta Cristina Fernández de Kirchner, Buenos Aires: Planeta, p. 2.

19 Rusconi, op cit.

20 Perfil (2020) Graciana Peñafort y Nelson Castro, debate sobre lawfare y periodismo, Mar. 15, https://bit.ly/3dglrIA.

21 Azar, Indiana Rocío y Tavares da Motta, Luiza (2020) Violência de gênero no Lawfare: uma análise dos casos Dilma Rousseff e Cristina Fernández de Kirchner, en Aguilar Viana, Ana Cristina (ed.) Pesquisa, Gênero & Diversidade Memórias do III Encontro de Pesquisa por/ de/sobre Mulheres, vol. I, pp. 269-271.

Marielle Franco in Brazil,[22] and even traditional military coups, as in Bolivia,[23] are still in force, these options are secondary to the mechanisms of lawfare. In other words, lawfare replaces the direct use of force and "physical death" as the main option and, instead, operates at the institutional level with a view to the "legal and political death" of the dissident. The "political death" seeks to erode the public image and the electoral flow of the judicially persecuted, delegitimize them and turning them into the cause of all the country's ills, the case of Cristina Fernández de Kirchner in Argentina being exemplary.[24] The "legal death" seeks to disqualify the persecuted from the legal possibility of participating in politics, as in the cases of the former Vice President of Argentina, Amado Boudou, or the former President of Bolivia, Evo Morales.[25] In extreme cases, this legal death may even require the effective imprisonment of renowned political leaders, as shown by the case of the former president of Brazil and author of the prologue of this book, Ignacio "Lula" da Silva, or that of the Argentine social leader Milagro Sala.[26]

The actions of the judiciary are necessarily intertwined with those of other actors, including the intelligence services, generally conceived as auxiliaries of justice at the disposal of the order of the day, and corporate power or real

---

22 Miranda, David (2019) "Who ordered Marielle Franco's murder?" *The Guardian*, Mar. 14, https://www.theguardian.com/commentisfree/2019/mar/14/marielle-franco-murder -brazil.

23 Zaffaroni, Raúl (2019b) "Entrevista a Eugenio Raúl Zaffaroni Bolivia: Golpe de Estado al presidente indio" – Por Conrado Yasenza, *La Tecla Eñe*, Nov. 19, https://lateclaenerevista .com/entrevista-a-eugenio-raul-zaffaroni-bolivia-golpe-de-estado-al-presidente-indio -por-conrado-yasenza/.

24 Infobae (2021) Después del sobreseimiento en "dólar futuro," qué causas tiene Cristina Kirchner y en qué estado se encuentran, Abr. 14, https://www.infobae.com/politica/2021 /04/14/despues-del-sobresimiento-en-dolar-futuro-que-causas-tiene-cristina-kirchner-y -en-que-estado-se-encuentran/.

25 Ámbito (2021a) Amado Boudou: "Me gustaría que se revierta la imposibilidad de ejercer cargos públicos," Jul. 23, https://www.ambito.com/politica/amado-boudou/me-gustaria -que-se-revierta-la-imposibilidad-ejercer-cargos-publicos-n5230839; EFE (2020) Un tribunal rechaza el pedido de habilitar la candidatura de Evo Morales al Senado, Sep. 8, https://www.efe.com/efe/america/politica/un-tribunal-rechaza-el-pedido-de-habilitar -la-candidatura-evo-morales-al-senado/20000035-4337320.

26 CELS (2021) Milagro Sala: 5 años de detención arbitraria y criminalización de la protesta social, Ene. 1, https://www.cels.org.ar/web/2021/01/milagro-sala-5-anos-de-detencion -arbitraria-y-criminalizacion-de-la-protesta-social/; Santoro, Antonio Eduardo Ramires y Tavares, Natália Lucero Frias (2019) *Lawfare* Brasileiro, Belo Horizonte: Editora D'Placido; TSE (2018) TSE indefere pedido de registro de candidatura de Lula à Presidência da República, Sep. 1, https://www.tse.jus.br/imprensa/noticias-tse/2018/Setembro/tse-indef ere-pedido-de-registro-de-candidatura-de-lula-a-presidencia-da-republica.

power at the local and global level. They are the main beneficiaries of the country, assuming a political course aligned with the neoliberal agenda and of the interruption of social justice programs that entail fiscal "spending" and strengthening of national sovereignty. In this sense, U.S. interests have always been key in the destiny of Latin American politics. Rusconi explains that under the regional sponsorship of the United States, criminal law serves to discipline political processes; the message implicit in every criminal case is "Never again will there be a popular or center-left government."[27]

In other words, these processes are not arbitrary. In line with Operation Condor of the 1970s, they share a dominant message, promoted and supported by the United States, and oriented towards governments of a certain political spectrum.[28] This is not new. Punitivity has always been an instrument of social verticalization that allowed Europe to colonize the Global South and now, by (il)legal means, it paves the way for those who want to keep Latin America the "backyard" of the empire. Indeed, the role of reported corruption as a major regional problem is framed by the adjustment and privatization plans promoted by the international financial institutions (International Monetary Fund, World Bank, Inter-American Development Bank) and U.S. bilateral agencies in Latin America (the U.S. Agency for International Development). In country assessment documents containing "recommendations" and in the processes of training local leaders through "good practices," these agencies include:

> the narrative of "corruption" as an (unavoidable) evil of the public sector and the State. This corruption must be extirpated from the State by appealing to the private sector (efficiency and transparency) to displace the "logic" of the public sector, associated with waste and mismanagement of "politicians" (read: militants, officials with a background in political parties), and by betting on the training of technicians (supposedly apolitical).[29]

In this framework, the recommendations on justice reforms are part of the battle against the "inefficiency of the state" and the prosecution for "corruption" of those leaders who favored interventionist policies and the expansion of the state against the instructions of "efficiency" and privatization.[30] The US

27   Rusconi, op cit.

28   Bielsa, Rafael y Peretti, Pedro (2019) op cit, p. 18.

29   Romano, Silvina (2019) *Lawfare: Guerra Judicial y Neoliberalismo en América Latina*, Buenos Aires: Mármol-Izquierdo.

30   Romano, op cit.

government in particular has tended to expand the Foreign Corrupt Practices Act (FCPA) as a pillar of its foreign policy, even though it does not necessarily apply it at home.[31]

Of course, the power of the North does not operate alone. As Raúl Zaffaroni points out,[32] lawfare is the result of the combination of interests of international and local financial powers. This mixture of U.S. interference and local interests were obvious in the case against Lula. Conversations leaked by *The Intercept* revealed the collaboration between Brazilian judge Sergio Moro and U.S. officials, evident as well in the regulations under which the case was registered: the FCPA. Indeed, the case against Lula da Silva has its origins in a process initiated by the U.S. Department of Justice against the Brazilian transnational corporation Odebrecht in December 2016 for works carried out in U.S. territory. Within that framework, the United States requested the collaboration of the courts in those Latin American countries where the company had performed work.[33] Meanwhile, in Argentina, Wikileaks cable 1222 revealed a meeting between the then Head of Government of the City of Buenos Aires and later president of the country under the neoliberal agenda, Mauricio Macri, and staff of the U.S. ambassador, in which the latter criticized the dismissal of criminal charges filed against social activist Luis D'Elía, who would later be imprisoned as the result of lawfare cases.[34]

Added to all this is the role of think tanks, non-governmental organizations financed by business groups, which produce reports and information aimed at influencing public opinion and reaffirming the accusations disseminated by the media. Large international organizations, such as Transparency International, intervene by defining the categories of "corruption" and "transparency" from the perspective of the Global North and using them themselves to measure countries by their own criteria.

Now, why an anglicism? Are there other concepts in the Spanish language that could replace the anglicism "lawfare?" The term "judicial warfare" is sometimes used, but it is problematic from the lessons learned from human rights organizations in Latin America. In the civil-military dictatorships of the 1970s

---

31   Koehler, Mike (2015) *The Uncomfortable Truths and Double Standards of Bribery Enforcement*, Fordham Law Review, v. 84, n. 525, https://ir.lawnet.fordham.edu/flr/vol84/iss2/8.

32   Zaffaroni, Raúl (2019a) Prólogo, en Romano, Silvina (ed.) *Lawfare: Guerra Judicial y Neoliberalismo en América Latina*, Buenos Aires: Mármol-Izquierdo, pp. 9–17.

33   Brasil Wire (2018) Lula's defence: New evidence shows illegal cooperation between United States & Lava Jato investigators, Mar. 16 https://www.brasilwire.com/lulas-defence-new-evidence-shows-illegal-cooperation-between-united-states-lava-jato-investigators/.

34   Estepa y Maisonnave 2019 op cit.

and particularly in Argentina, the term "dirty war" was used to describe the existence of two belligerent sides, in some way equivalent. However, there was no equal confrontation between leftist and military organizations, but rather a situation of state terrorism directed by the latter with the purpose of annihilating the former. In the same sense, there are not two equal sides in present-day Latin America either. Instead, lawfare is backed by monopolistic corporate and media powers, embassies and intelligence services. In a global geopolitical situation in which these concentrated powers are increasingly superior even to states,[35] it is evident that their capabilities cannot be equated to those of progressive leaders even while the latter hold office.

Another concept that appears to replace the anglicism is "soft coup" or "media-legal coup." Although it is clearer, it does not account for situations in which lawfare is used against leaders who are not in government (e.g., Milagro Sala), while it may also generate the misconception that the mechanism necessarily takes place at a specific moment (the coup) through a particularly explosive denunciation. Instead, in most cases, what happens is that several denunciations and accusations erode over time the political and legal life of the leader under attack (as evidenced by the case of Cristina Fernández de Kirchner in Argentina, with more than a dozen accumulated denunciations). Raúl Zaffaroni explains that genocides and massacres do not occur only from the mass annihilation of certain groups in moments of non-rights, but also take place in democratic contexts, by means of the daily actions taken by security forces against marginalized populations. In his words:

> *Unlike those we have seen and which occupy international attention, [drop-by-drop massacres] do not produce all the deaths at once. They produce them day by day ... The clearest example of this is the violence that Mexico is suffering today, where the* drop-by-drop massacre *is turning into an ordinary massacre, with a very high number of corpses.*[36]

In a similar sense, it is possible to propose that soft coups also occur "drop by drop," that is, through the daily accumulation of news, denunciations and testimonies that coincide in attacking a particular leader. A characteristic of this sort of coup is that it does not require particularly solid accusations, but instead accumulates over time in the slow drip of small cases that may even consist of frivolous accusations, without evidence, presented in spite of the

---

35   Davis, K., Fisher, A., Kingsbury, B. y Merry, S. (2015) *Governance by Indicators*, Oxford, Oxford University Press.

36   Zaffaroni, Raúl (2011) *La Cuestión Criminal*, Buenos Aires: Planeta, p. 306–7.

certainty of the legal impossibility of advancing in a prosecution. In this way, the drop-by-drop coup, through the presentation of a multiplicity of cases and accusations, makes it possible not only to overwhelm the citizenry with an abundance of data difficult to process and understand, but also to create the sensation that, in one way or another, it is impossible that with all these cases at stake there is not at least one that is "true." At the same time, the drop-by-drop coup also makes it possible for many other cards to remain in play that allow the media-judicial maneuver to continue, even when some of the cases are dismissed or declared null and void.

What, then, is lawfare or the drop-by-drop coup? It is a specific modality of selecting criminals that manifests itself through the manipulation of the media-judicial system at the initiative, or with the support of, national and global corporate powers in a two-dimensional process. Along one dimension, the political and legal death of progressive leaders is sought through the presentation and dissemination of various criminal charges, even when the accused have not committed crimes. And along the other, lawfare is used to save leaders functional to financial capitalism from that same political and legal death, even when they have in fact committed crimes.

In terms of lawfare, this value-based application of the law is reflected in the misuse of criminal law and criminal procedure. In the former, the misuse is evidenced in the application of open criminal types (e.g., conspiracy, treason, abuse of power), in the extensive application of criminal types (to the detriment of the principle of legality), and in the expansion of authorship and distribution of responsibility in the governmental hierarchical chain (to the detriment of the principle of innocent until proven guilty and the rule of law).

In the procedural field, lawfare and discretion in the application of the law are evidenced in the alteration of the rules of jurisdiction and the guarantee of due process (*forum shopping*); in the use of the figure of repentance (not to seek the truth, but to blame the target of criminal prosecution); wiretapping and other coercive measures within the private sphere, either without a court order or used in cases in which they were not ordered (to humiliate and not to clarify the facts); in the (ab)use of pretrial detention for reasons not legally provided for as residual links (even in cases that depended mostly on written evidence or public documents, and not on witnesses); and in the assessment of flimsy evidence (for example, copies of notebooks in the case against Fernández de Kirchner, or the invocation of private feelings instead of evidence in the case against Lula). As Rusconi summarizes, far from an objective law and judicial system, lawfare shows the selective manipulation of dogmatic and Law of criminal procedure:

It requires a state willing to carry out the tasks of illegal intelligence, communicational monopolies in charge of giving the appearance of legitimacy to the origin of the information, prosecutors and judges with double standards, generous acceptance of information that arrives surprisingly and anonymously, an indiscriminate use of preventive detention, multiplication to infinity of the same charges, a judge willing to associate himself to the persecution (forum shopping), an Executive Branch that shamelessly stipulates the agenda of docile judges and prosecutors, institutional bodies that are compliant with this strategy as prosecutors, judicial councils that protect partner judges and apply corrective measures to independent judges, official defense attorneys who turn a blind eye, noisy legislators who help the protective climate of those who join the illegitimate persecution, and a powerful embassy that contributes to the 'protectorate.'[37]

For all its encroachments on the rule of law, the issue of lawfare opens up relevant discussions for our democracies. In a reflection of what happened in Argentina with the media law,[38] the exposure of lawfare opens up the possibility of disproving the objective and a-valorative vision of law, and of making clear to the nation's citizens the political, discretionary, and selective role exercised by the law and the justice systems, which may serve as a first step toward change.

---

37   Rusconi op cit.

38   Guzmán, Víctor Humberto (2017) "Una 'ley de medios' en los medios. La Ley de Servicios de Comunicación Audiovisual argentina en el espacio público mediatizado," *Estudios sobre el Mensaje Periodístico*, v. 22, n. 2.

CHAPTER 1

The Destruction of Criminal Law

Eugenio Raúl Zaffaroni

1 The Tortuous Path of Criminal Law

Whether or not law is a science, it is certainly a task performed by jurists with a practical objective, namely, to offer judges a system for interpreting the law that allows them to issue predictable, non-contradictory sentences. Legal knowledge in criminal matters likewise responds to this objective. Judgments derive their power from the state; they are acts of the *polis*, that is, political acts in the broad and obviously non-partisan sense. Criminal law, in terms of its general political orientation, has followed a rather tortuous and often sinister historical path. Punitive or retributive power aims to regulate criminal law, and consists in the intervention of the state in certain conflicts, in which it leaves aside the injured party, since it assumes the role of the victim. This *confiscation, usurpation or expropriation of the victim* is what distinguishes retributive power from the various forms of true conflict resolution, such as restorative, conciliatory, rehabilitative, or assistance.[1]

In reality, the penal model does not resolve conflict, because, by leaving out one party, it puts the conflict itself on hold. Criminal law is not conflict resolution. Rather, it allows the state to intervene in the conflict from above. These days the agency[2] exercising this power is the police, but in the past there were other agencies, such as the Roman centurions who executed Jesus. The function of the state's punitivity is to hierarchically verticalize societies; in the Western tradition, the Roman Empire epitomized this model.

When Rome fell to the Germanic peoples, the punitivity of the state diminished, because the Germani tended to resolve conflicts by means of reparation or composition,[3] reserving punishment almost exclusively for cases of treason. However, in Europe the penal model returned with renewed force around the

---

1 Zaffaroni, Raúl (2011) *La Cuestión Criminal*, Buenos Aires: Planeta.
2 European police forces emerged in the late 18th and early 20th centuries. On current models of police organization, see David Bayley, *Modelos de actividad policial. Un análisis comparativo internacional,* Buenos Aires, 2010.
3 Cfr. Eberhard Schmidt, *Einführung in die Geschite der deutschen Strafrechtspflege,* Göttingen, 1951.

twelfth century, when the lord or *dominus* began once again to proclaim *the victim is me*. The jurists of that time were quick to legitimize this punitivity as an indispensable weapon in the struggle against a fearsome enemy, in this case Satan and his female agents, the witches,[4] giving rise to a genocide that did not invent but certainly reaffirmed misogyny, patriarchy and the subhumanization of half the human species. Ever since, for almost a millennium now, punitivity has been seeking to free itself from every limitation, always invoking the threatening and destructive presence of more or less *cosmic* or *universal* enemies, which it describes as imminent and massive dangers so powerful that they cannot be stopped without recourse to the unlimited exercise of punishment. It could be said that penal law *satanizes*, rather than merely demonizes, certain human groups, for *Satan* in Hebrew means precisely *the enemy.*[5]

Throughout the last millennium, most real or imagined social evils were not only satanized in accordance with the cultural values of the era, but also magnified to a cosmic level. Rational solutions were therefore inadequate. The only way to neutralize the evil was by annihilating a more or less extensive category of human being. The magnification of evils has always been a way to legitimize assassinations. The evils satanized change according to their historical, cultural and political circumstances, and, taken as a whole, they form a nonsensical chain as varied as it is disconcerting: witches, heretics, indigenous peoples, Africans, Asians, Jews, Christians, Islamics, Buddhists, gays, syphilis, communism, capitalism, the bourgeoisie, alcoholism, drug addiction, degeneration, bastardization, contamination of the race, and many others that continue to be fabricated according to the society's ability to generate collective paranoias.[6]

Some of these satanizations would eventually legitimize the massacre of millions of people, leaving far more murder victims than the sum total of individually committed homicides.[7] But while the latter type of murder understandably terrifies us, the state-initiated killings "justified" by the satanization of a collective "enemy" seldom produce the same effect. The legitimization of this lethal and uncontrolled exercise of punitivity culminated in the argument that the power to determine the enemy to be annihilated was the very essence

---

4   Cfr. Kurt Baschwitz, *Hexen und Hexenprozesse*, München, 1966.
5   Cfr. Reiner Braun, *Teufelsglaube und Heilige Schirft*, en Georg Schwaiger (ed.) "Teufelsglaube und Hezenprozesse," Hamburg, 2007, p. 17.
6   Cfr. Jean Delumeau, *El miedo en Occidente*, Madrid, 2012; Luigi Zoja, *Paranoia. La locura que hace la historia*, Buenos Aires, 2013.
7   Cfr. Wayne Morrison, *Criminology, Civilisation and the New World Order*, New York, 2006.

of politics,[8] that is to say, that politics was criminal and justly so, because that was its essence, that was its purpose.

2   The "Founding Fathers" of Good Criminal Law

But it was not all bad news in criminal law. Beginning in the 18th century in Europe, when, in an effort to obtain social hegemony, a class of industrialists, merchants and bankers challenged a lethargic aristocracy, a series of thinkers, philosophers and jurists upheld the need to impose rational limits on punitivity. Their efforts gave rise to an enlightened and liberal theory of criminal law, one pursued either by deductive and rationalist or by empirical means, in accordance with the two currents that converged in the philosophical Enlightenment.[9]

For all their shortcomings – most obviously the fact that the limitations of punishment were intended only for their own societies, and not for the subjects they had colonized, who would remain enslaved on the grounds that they were "inferior" – one must nevertheless recognize that these thinkers sustained a strong liberating impulse against the absolutism of the unbridled punitivity that had previously held sway. In the field of criminal law, there emerged specialists such as Cesare Beccaria[10] and Pietro Verri[11] in Milan, Josef von Sonnenfels[12] in Austria, Karl Hommel[13] and Paul Feuerbach[14] in Germany, Manuel de Lardizabal[15] in Spain, William Blackstone[16] and Jeremy Bentham[17] in England, William Godwin[18] in the United States, Gaetano Filangieri[19] and

---

8   Carl Schmitt, *El concepto de lo político*, México, 1985.
9   Cfr. Ernst Cassirer, *Filosofía de la Ilustración*, México, 1972.
10   Cesare Beccaria, *Dei delitti e delle pene*, 1764.
11   Pietro Verri, *Observaciones sobre la tortura*, trans. de Manuel de Rivacoba, Buenos Aires, 1977.
12   Josef von Sonnenfels, *Über die Abschaffung der Tortur*, Zürich, 1775.
13   Karl Ferdinand Hommel, *Philosophische Gedanken über Criminalrecht*, Braslau, 1784.
14   About his life and his works, Gustav Radbruch, *Paul Johann Anselm Feuerbach. Ein Juristenleben*, Springer, 1934.
15   Manuel de Lardizábal y Uribe, *Discurso sobre las penas contraído a las leyes penales de España, para facilitar su reforma*, preliminary study by Manuel de Rivacoba y Rivacoba in colaboration with José Luis Guzmán Dalbora, Vitoria, 2001.
16   William Blackstone, *Commentaires sur les lois angleises*, París, 1823; *Comentario sul Codice Penale d'Inghilterra*, Milano, 1815.
17   Cfr. a complete bibliography and information on Leon Radzinowicz, *A History of English Criminal Law and its Administration from 1750*, London, 1948, I, 355 y ss.
18   William Godwin, *An Enquiry concerning political justice and its influence on general virtue and happiness*, Dublin, 1793.
19   Gaetano Filangieri, *Scienza della Legislazione*, Firenze, 1864.

Francesco Pagano[20] in Naples, and Melo Freire[21] in Portugal. Thus began the development of a tradition of criminal law dedicated to imposing more or less rational limits on the exercise of punitivity, that is, to directing judges to limit its exercise.

Since that historical moment, theorists of so-called *liberal* criminal law (liberal in the healthy political sense of the expression, as opposed to the economistically reductive *neoliberalism* of today) have proclaimed themselves defenders of so-called *legal guarantees* now enshrined in constitutions and in international law,[22] guarantees that limit the punitivity regulated by law. In general, these jurists seek to legitimize a degree of *legal* punitivity, and to eliminate those punitive measures deemed irrational or excessive. Unaware of the real functions that punitivity performs in their societies, they ascribe to punitivity and punishment purely imaginary functions.[23] They tend to hallucinate states that do not actually exist (the Kantian *ethical*, the Hegelian *rational*, the Krausian *moralizing*, etc.), without realizing that, by envisioning these different functions of punishment, what they are really discussing are models of statehood. In other words, they treat as matters of penal law problems that are in reality some of the most difficult questions of political theory.

But these arguments also obscure the fact that punitivity is not confined to the court circuit. A kind of punitivity known as *informal* is amply exercised by agencies operating independently of any judicial control, namely, the police, as well as in the deformation or perversion of other institutions (psychiatric, asylums, shelters for children and adolescents, etc.) and even by individuals (paramilitaries, parapolice, vigilantes, self-defense groups).

The theoretical disregard of *informal punitivity* is perhaps more understandable in the Northern Hemisphere than in Latin America, where it is exercised to a greater extent, in the form of sentences without trial, forced disappearances, police torture, imprisonment in jails already at double or triple their capacity and controlled by prisoner gangs, and extortion involving "tax collection" by entities other than the state. Episodes of this nature in the Global North – at least when they are repeated – usually give rise to scandals,

---

20   Francesco Mario Pagano, *Principi del Codice Penale*, Napoli, 1803.

21   Pascoal José de Melo Freire, *Institutionum Juris Criminalis Lusitani, Liber Singularis*, Coimbra, 1842.

22   On the integration of these rights, from a new perspective, Peter Häberle, *Sobre el Principio de la Paz. La "cultura de la paz." El tópico de la teoría constitucional universal*, Bs. As., 2021.

23   In general, the theories are reiterated according to the classification that dates back to Anton Bauer, *Die Warnungstheorie nebst einer Darstellung aller Strafrechtstheorien*, Göttingen, 1830.

but in the South, despite the efforts of regional human rights organizations, they are normalized and even hidden by the monopolized media, who will go so far as to justify them by claiming that a *firm hand* is necessary in the fight against crime.

3   The Positive Function of Criminal Law

In any event, even with these flaws, criminal lawyers have every reason to be proud of their function as containers of punitivity, for what they can truly point to as their contribution to humanity is precisely the provision of systems that allow judges to curtail the exercise of punishment. Indeed, if judges did not restrain this exercise, punitivity, a purely political act akin to war,[24] would extend without limit and culminate in genocide. Indeed, every genocide that occurred in the last century was committed by agencies that, endowed with the manifest function of preventing or repressing crimes, ended up committing the most serious crimes of all.

It is said that genocides are committed by states. This is true, but if we ask ourselves who were the material executors, we will see that in every instance, they were the police (the Gestapo, the SS, the KGB, etc.). True, some were also committed by armed forces, but these were no longer performing wartime or national defense functions, and had instead been reduced to the role of internal police. It may be objected that in many cases they did not themselves perform the massacres, but rather allowed them to take place by action or omission, as when they released prisoners to go off and kill Armenians they found along the way,[25] or when they indifferently witnessed the butchery in Rwanda.[26] The larger point is that when punitivity is deprived of any juridical restraint, it expands and becomes criminal.

---

24   This parallel was pointed out in the 19th century by Tobias Barreto, *Algumas idéias sobre lo chamado fundamento do direito de punir* (1886), en "Obras completas," Sergipe, 1926, T. V.

25   Cfr. Vahakn N. Dadrian, *The history of the Armenian Genocide*, Oxford, 1997; Donald Bloxham, *Il "grande gioco" del genocidio*, Milano, 2007; Marcello Flores, *Il genocidio degli armeni*, Bologna, 2006.

26   Cfr. Jacques Sémelin, *Purificar y destruir. Usos políticos de las masacres y genocidios,* San Martín, 2013.

4   Forgetting the "Founding Fathers"

It is true that criminal law did not entirely follow the ideological path traced by the old *liberals* (in the positive political sense of the expression). It often wandered off the path and ended up legitimizing an uncontrolled and criminal exercise of punitivity. From the late nineteenth century until the end of the Second World War, criminal law forgot about its liberal founding fathers, opting instead for a mode of racist reductionism that criminologists called *Positivism*, which legitimized the punishment of persons, not acts. Positivism did not wish to punish the crimes actually committed, but rather those that the police presumed the "criminal type" might commit in the future, even if he had never actually undertaken or even imagined them.

Criminal law also repudiated its liberal founding fathers in the worst possible way when it bowed to and incorporated the values of a supposedly superior Aryan race that called itself a *community of the people* (*Volksgemeinschaft*). In some instances, it took refuge in the methodology of this very particular valuational idealism; in others it simply fell into an institutionalized irrationalism, ceding to administrative law the task of eliminating millions of people.[27] Although with much less lethal effect, criminal law also legitimized the hallucinated war of *national security* between *East and West*,[28] which claimed hundreds of thousands of victims in Central America and many thousands in South America.

These episodes are now generally dismissed as part of *shameful criminal law*, the history of which also includes the inquisitions and crimes of colonialism and neocolonialism, which also tend to be forgotten. Criminal law, preferring to display only its positive side, is embarrassed by these deviations and would rather hide them, much as an illustrious family tries to hide the smuggler, pirate, slave trader or "Indian killer" included among its ancestors. Criminal law seeks to highlight its unquestionably beneficial contribution, i.e., its function of limiting the exercise of punitivity. In this sense, criminal law proclaims itself the heir of the *liberal fathers*, since no institute or academy honors the name of the great inquisitor Torquemada;[29] even the names of the theoreticians of the Inquisition are remembered only by historians[30] – for criminal

---

27   This was the nature of Nazi racial laws Cfr. Wilhelm Stuckart – Hans Globke, *Kommentare zud deutschen Rassengesetze*, Berlin, 1936.

28   Cfr. Marie-Monique Robin, *Escuadrones de la muerte. La escuela francesa*, Bs. As., 2005.

29   Cfr. Franco Ingegneri, *Torquemada. Atrocità e segreti dell' 'Inquisizione spagnola*, Milano, 1966.

30   See the authors compiled by Abbiati-Agnoletto-Lazzati en *La stregneria. Diavoli stregue, inquisitori dal trecento al settecento*, Milano, 1991, none of these names appear in current

lawyers they are buried in oblivion. Nowadays in the universities, the history of criminal law[31] tends to be undervalued, as if it were merely entertainment for curious antiquarians and not part of a branch of knowledge that is in its essence cultural, historical, and political.

But there is no limit to the perverse and paranoid imagination that hypertrophies any societal problem in order to unleash an unrestrained punitivity. Surprisingly, punitivity has never managed to neutralize any of the evils whose dangers it has aggrandized to the incredible level of *cosmic*. Some ceased to be evil, others never were to begin with, others were resolved by different means, and still others have never been resolved by anyone, and have yet to destroy the world. Sociology has long referred to institutional functions by classifying them as *manifest* or *latent*,[32] that is, either something they claim to do or something they actually do. In this sense, it is evident that in all cases, punitivity has laid claim to manifest functions that had nothing to do with its real or latent ones. In other words, they have been frauds. It is striking that, for a millennium now, time and again, human beings – including jurists themselves – have let themselves be scammed by these massive swindles. At the level of the individual, we consider someone who repeatedly falls victim to the same ruse supremely unintelligent, and react to him with a mixture of pity and indignation.

But criminal law itself, by pretending to forget its history so as to hide its unworthy ancestors, and universities, by hiding it from the students they train, do nothing but train them in naiveté. Ignoring or underestimating the history of a millennium of scams only prepares them to fall victim to the next ruse. And yet this path seems to be dangerously insisted upon, and even the faults of some of our contemporaries are often disguised when they slip in some overly enabling concept of punitivity, generally by discrediting another colleague considered too *liberal* – which is an inveterate custom among scholars of the subject –, although later, the criticized one is usually vindicated, sometimes after he has already left this world.

It is not at all healthy for criminal law to consider itself only the daughter of the *liberal fathers*, while forgetting that it is the granddaughter of the Inquisition[33] and that it had some dangerously deviant cousins as legitimizers

criminal law manuals and treatises on criminal law, i.e., legal science has forgotten or denied them.

31   Cfr. Klaus Marxen, *Strafrecht nach der Überwindung zweier Unrechtsregime in Deutschland*, en "Fest. 200 Jahre Juristische Fakultät der Humboldt-Universität zu Berlin," 2010, p. 209.

32   Cfr. Robert K Merton, *Teoría y estructura sociales*, México, 1970, p. 71.

33   Cfr. Our *Friedrich Spee: el padre de la criminología crítica*, preliminary study to the "Cautio Criminalis," Buenos Aires, 2017.

of genocides. For today's jurists, *true criminal law* refers only to that which limits the exercise of punitivity, and that is indeed true. Unpleasant memories tend to be buried, but by forgetting *shameful criminal law* one risks repeating the same deviations. The criminal law of the old *liberal fathers* was a criminal law of struggle against the uncontrolled exercise of punitivity, and this struggle, but with new *satanizations,* continues to the present day.

5   The Dismemberment of Criminal Law

The false belief that punitivity is only exercised by judges, and that it will operate precisely as jurists imagine it should be exercised, puts *true criminal law* – of which penalists are rightly proud – at risk, and paves the way for its destruction. Incredibly, many law practitioners sustain this false belief in good faith, and even convince many judges.

This confusion is the prolog to the dismemberment of *true criminal law,* whose dismembered remains are then assembled in crude *collages* that legitimize the discourses of punitivity, at times somewhat limited, at others completely uncontrolled, giving rise to the renewal of *shameful criminal law,* which has always fulfilled the sad function of legitimizing that what should be restrained. Generally, when uncontrolled, unrestrained punitivity expands and commits the worst crimes, unleashing reactions of indignation and resistance that culminate in disaster and its subsequent containment, the penal law of the post-catastrophic moment modestly hides those *collages* and tries to forget them.

The characteristic of selectivity in the exercise of all punitivity was revealed by criminal sociology a long time ago[34] and can be verified by reviewing the composition of any penal population in the world; certain demographics are always overrepresented, according to the place and the historical moment.[35] In Latin America, the dominant group is young men of color with fragile personalities, from precarious neighborhoods, with little or no education or job

---

34   For an overview, see Massimo Pavarini, *Introduzione a ... la criminologia,* Firenze, 1980; Lola Aniyar de Castro – Rodrigo Codino, *Manual de Criminología Sociopolítica,* Buenos Aires, 2013.

35   The "south" and the "north" are not geographic locations, so penal selectivity also has effects in the "north," where there are pieces of "south, " cfr. Boaventura de Souza Santos, *Um discurso sobre as ciências,* São Paulo, 2008. Those preferentially selected in the "north" are not the same as those in the "south," but they exist at both extremes, just as the exclusion of immigrants in the "north" cannot be ignored today. (cfr. Alessandro Dal Lago, *Nonpersone. L'esclusione dei migranti in una società globale,* Milano, 1999).

training, and who have been accused of crimes against property or the distribution of toxic substances. Most are in pretrial detention awaiting trial.[36] Certainly the judges are not selecting this group, although they do contribute to it. It suffices to observe the front steps of any courthouse to see that the prisoners emerge handcuffed from police vehicles. That is to say, they were not selected by the judges, but by the police. The judges only decide whether they should be imprisoned.

This function of *traffic light* or luminous signal for the circulation of formal punitivity is what weakens *shameful criminal law* to varying degrees, but when it reaches extreme situations, not of ineffective control but of legitimizing a lack of control, judges and judicial officials cease to be such, and become clowns submissive to police mandates, like Roland Freisler, who insulted and spat on the accused,[37] or like the prosecutor Andrei Vishinski in the Stalinist purges of the thirties.[38]

Forgetfulness has meant that, for many today, these names no longer mean anything, because these bad memories are omitted from the academic training of our law students. The truth is that the victims of the Nazi genocide (millions of Jews, Gypsies, dissidents, and gays) were not sent to forced labor and death by judges, but by the police. That totalitarian state did not apply any criminal law against them, but exercised a so-called *administrative law of racial hygiene police*, against which the shameless jurists said nothing and, naturally, neither did the judges trained by them. The fact of the matter is that whenever the *real* criminal law is dismembered, the *shameless* one that replaces it establishes its own limits, paving the way for its irrelevance by alleged exercises of so-called police administrative rights.

6   Conditions for the Creation of "Shameful Criminal Law:" The Great Swindle

In order to legitimize this uncontrolled police power and its crimes, it is necessary to generate enormous fear, inventing the *cosmic evil* previously discussed and attributing it to an *enemy* whom, naturally, must be annihilated,

36   This trend was detected throughout the region four decades ago and continues, see Carranza/Mora/Houed/Zaffaroni, *El preso sin condena en América Latina y el Caribe*, San José, 1983.

37   In this regard, see the work of Gerhard Pauli y Thomas Vormbaum (eds.), *Justiz und Nationalsozialismus. Kontinuität uns Diskontinuität*, Berlin, 2003.

38   Arcadi Vaksberg, *Vychinski. Le Procureur de Staline, Les grands procés de Moscou*, París, 1991.

no opposition brooked. Anyone who presumes to oppose this supposedly redemptive annihilation of the enemy, or who questions the neutralization of the *universal evil* that instills panic or paralyzing terror, is either an enemy or a *useful idiot,* simply because by challenging the *cosmic* or universal character of evil, he also challenges the power of those manipulating punitivity for objectives of political and economic domination, that is, the swindlers who invent evil in order to manipulate through fear.

For the inquisitors, who burned women with singular determination all over Europe, the worst enemies were those who questioned the power of witches.[39] The Argentine dictatorship claimed that human rights defenders were terrorists, and one of the pepetrators of that genocide went so far as to say that after the enemies they would deal with those who were not so radicalized but who followed that enemy line. Right now, in some Latin American countries, human rights defenders and journalists, stigmatized as *subversives,* *communists* and even *guerrillas,* are being killed. In all these cases, those who hold political power promote iron options, without intermediate positions, since the choice is always between unbridled police power and a *cosmic evil. The City of God* or *the City of the Evil One,* said the Inquisitors; *Rome* or *Moscow,* said Mussolini; Stalin pitted the *dictatorship of the proletariat* against *exploitative capitalism*; Latin American national security dictatorships propose an opposition between *Westerners and Christians,* or *International Communism.* Nevertheless, it must be emphasized that whenever punitivity overflowed and the legal power of containment diminished or disappeared, legitimized by some version of *shameful* criminal law, that power was used for the benefit of different interests, never to solve the problems that it aggravated and that it loudly claimed to be struggling to solve.

Over the course of the last two centuries, those interests often became those of states that sought to dominate the world, justifying themselves with systems of paranoid ideas about their respective *enemies* and *cosmic evils,* as well as about the promises of their opponents, that is, of their *future paradises* or *cosmic goods.* Thus, in the 19th century, the *cosmic evil* was *degeneration* due to the interruption of the evolution that allowed the brain to develop, the enemies were the *inferiors* (colonized and delinquents), and the *cosmic good* was the general growth of the brain, which would better flourish after the *weak inferiors* were eliminated through *natural selection.* According to these genocidal ideas, based on pseudo-scientific biology and disseminated by the power of the moment (Great Britain), the weak and colonized should die (*Spencerian*

---

39   Cfr. Heinrich Kramer – Jakob Sprenger, *Malleus Maleficarum,* Rosario, 2021,Chapter I.

neocolonialist racism),[40] and the infectious cells of the social organism, that is, the *small brains* that by accident appeared in the midst of the society of *big brains*, were also to be eliminated.

This gave rise to the *shameful* criminal law of racist police *dangerousness*[41] that a century ago was taught throughout Latin America, and which today no jurist wishes to remember. Many of those dour personages whose portraits, framed in gilded baroque, still hang on the walls of our universities, disseminated these ideas, ideas as false as they were simplistic and genocidal. In the 20th century there were others who believed that their brains were already developed and that the *cosmic evil* now consisted in the *contamination* of their blood with that of *inferiors* (Jews, blacks, gypsies, Indians). In this case, the *cosmic good* was the re-establishment of the *pure Aryan race*, which would come into its own after all the contaminating enemies were annihilated.[42]

According to these genocidal ideas spread in the *counter-power* of the moment (Nazi Germany), it was necessary to kill all the polluters. This would be done by the *administrative law* of *racial cleansing*, reserving for the shameful criminal law the task of eliminating the minority of *degenerate Aryans* who, with their criminal intentions, revealed a certain degree of contamination. Thus, shameful criminal law eliminated the already *contaminated*, while the administrative police law eliminated the *contaminators*. This was the Nazi variable of shameful criminal law.[43]

In the same century, there was no shortage of those who believed themselves heirs of the Roman Empire and set themselves the task of rebuilding it, with *cosmic evil* now defined as *disobedience to the state*, understood as a synthesis of past, present and future generations.[44] The cosmic good was the order imposed by the state after disciplining or eliminating dissidents, that is, those unable to understand that they did not matter as individuals, but only as part of this spiritual, superior and all-encompassing entity, the state-society-nation (all confused) to which unconditional obedience[45] was due. According to this idea of the totalitarian state, it was necessary to reaffirm the will of

---

40   The penal version of this spenciarinism was *Lombrosianism*, which stigmatized the leaders of the Paris Commune and the anarchists, cf. Cesare Lombroso/R. Laschi, *Le crime politique et les révolutions*, Paris, 1892; C. Lombroso, *Gli anarchici*, Torino, 1894.

41   The penal version of this current in Enrico Ferri, *Principii di Diritto Criminale*, Torino, 1928.

42   Thus, Helmut Nicolai, *Die rassengesetzliche Rechtslehre. Grundzüge einer nationlsozialisztische Rechtsphilosophie*, München, 1932.

43   Georg Dahm, *Der Ehrenschutz der Gemeinschaft*, en "Fest. F. Gleispach," Berlin-Leipzig, 1936.

44   Alfredo Rocco, *Relazione al Re*, in "Gazzetta Ufficiale" 26 october 1930.

45   Cfr. H. Donnedieu de Vabres, *La crise moderne du Droit Pénal, La politique criminelle des États autoritaires*, París, 1938.

the punitive state expressed in its laws, and to recognize as the only free and valid will that which was obedient to the state, understood at the same time as society and *synthesis of the nation*. This was the fascist variable of *shameful criminal law*.[46]

And many others believed that it was necessary to change everything to achieve the perfect equality demanded by the proletarian class: the *cosmic evil* was capitalism, the bourgeoisie were the enemies, and the *cosmic good* was the egalitarian socialist society that would be obtained only after eliminating the bourgeoisie and creating the *new man*. Since for that to happen it was necessary to eradicate not only the bourgeoisie but also bourgeois habits from society, the proletarians had to temporarily establish a transitory dictatorship until the new man emerged. This was the Stalinist variable of *shameful* criminal law.[47]

Unfortunately, these *cosmic goods* did not materialize in the promised *paradises* of big-headed races, nor in a new Roman empire, nor in the perfect egalitarian society, but rather in wars that left millions dead and involved atrocious crimes against humanity. Nor, in the seventies of the last century, did the so-called doctrine of *national security*, generated by French colonialism and disseminated among the leaders of the Latin American armed forces from the School of the Americas in Panama,[48] lead us to the *cosmic good* of their Western and Christian civilization. Instead it left us with hundreds of thousands of dead in the region, through the work of an uncontrolled punitivity that supposedly saved us from a non-existent hell.

The truth is that, as we have pointed out before, the juridical scribes of all these criminal political powers dismembered *true* penal law, and then stuck its bleeding limbs in the sad theses and dark, confused appendices of their hallucinatory political paranoias about *enemies, cosmic evils,* and delusionary *absolute goods*. The *collages* of speeches covering up the genocides and atrocious crimes of neocolonial racism, Nazism, Fascism, Stalinism and National Security were nothing but the crude jumbles – some not very ingenious – made from the dismembered limbs of *true criminal law*.

---

46   The difference between the shameful Nazi and Fascist versions was very clearly explained by the Nazi penalist Georg Dahm, *Nationalsozialistisches und faschistisches Strafrecht*, Berlin, 1935.

47   Cfr. T. Napolitano, *Le nuove teorie penali nella Rusia sovietica*, en "Scuola Positiva," 1931; H. Donnedieu de Vabres, op. Cit.

48   Cfr. Marie-Monique Robin, *Escuadrones de la muerte*, op cit.

7   Dismemberment, Decapitation and Recomposition of
       Criminal Law

To be clear, it has always been possible to dissemble or feign judicial and doctrinal indifference, so as to avoid openly aligning oneself with the *shameful*
criminal law of the time. There are always those who know that *this too shall
pass,* and that it is very hard and even dangerous to assume the responsibility of
dismembering *true* criminal law, because at some point they may be called to
account for this dismemberment. In order to evade responsibility and cultivate
indifference and a low profile, there is no shortage of seemingly technocratic,
aseptic, elegant and sophisticated theoretical elaborations that merely *decapi-
tate true criminal law*, depriving it of its function of containing punitivity.

This *decapitation* can be carried out coarsely with the ax or finely with the
scalpel, but in all cases, neither social reality nor, especially, the selectivity of
punitivity are allowed to penetrate the theoretical construction of criminal
law. Extremely useful for this purpose are idealistic theories of knowledge,
appeals to imaginary ethical or rational states and, above all, the reduction of
juridical logic to a purely normative logic whose objective is limited to avoid-
ing contradictions, that is, one that remains in the pure terrain of what ought
to be, without ever asking questions about what it really is.

This decapitated criminal law is perfectly functional for judicial bureaucra-
cies that prefer to ignore their periods of uncontrolled punitivity, who swim
blithely through reality while claiming not to notice that the waters that sustain them also keep corpses afloat; indeed, they concern themselves with the
corpses only when their ability to sail on with total indifference is somehow
impeded. And, once the terror has passed, this attitude often allows them to
present themselves as defenders of law and legality.

Notwithstanding, *true criminal law*, which permits judges to contain and
delimit punitivity, somehow reconstructs itself after every s*hameful* episode
because it possesses a virtue proper to certain mythological beings: it regener-
ates itself from its decapitated body, from the dismembered pieces detached
from the *collages*. This extraordinary virtue derives from the liberating impulse
nestled deep within every human being who aspires to be considered and
treated as a person, an impulse towards freedom that cannot be extinguished.
But if Eros is never absent, neither does Thanatos disappear: if, after true criminal law has been reconstructed, the tricks of the demonization scam are not
noticed in time, then the grim bearers of axes, saws and scalpels reemerge onto
the scene. Thus, *dismemberment* and *decapitation* on the one hand, and *recon-
struction* on the other, seem to be the *corsi e ricorsi* of the dynamics of criminal

law, a long pendulum swing between *true* criminal law and its dismembered, decapitated, *shameful* variants.

After every uncontrolled punitivity catastrophe, penal law tends to hide the version of *shameful* criminal law that legitimized it, piously filing it away in the attic with forgotten suits and dresses, or in the sewers where one of Umberto Eco's characters would hide his corpses.[49] This is the fate of the dismembered versions. The decapitated ones, however, often manage to camouflage themselves, claiming a neutral and technocratic sterility; it is always easier to reattach a head to a body than gather up its dismembered remains. The butchers and their inventions are inevitably archived away into oblivion. Occasionally, as pieces of the *real* criminal law are recovered from their *collages*, they are partially rescued from oblivion, until someone recalls what the *collage* in its entirety was like and modestly suggests that we forget the whole thing, and not stir up the past or ruin the party with bad memories.

8   The Current Conditions for the Construction of "Shameful" Criminal Law

In recent decades, the supra-state power of financial capital has elevated the distributive policy of states to the status of a *cosmic evil*, generating a veritable idolatry of the false market god, according to which all human life (marriage, children, career, friendships, etc.) is determined in compliance with the *law of supply and demand.*[50]

Its *enemy* is redistributive policy, its *cosmic evil* is every attempt by the state to intervene on behalf of the most disadvantaged, and its *cosmic good* is the sovereignty of the market, which will allow the rich to get richer until their wealth trickles down to those below and reaches everyone.[51] According to this very poor ideology[52] that usurps the name of liberalism, the state should be limited to a police function, and it is even proposed to privatize it, in an *anarcho-capitalism* that would effectively dissolve the state into a sad,

---

49   We refer to his work *Il cimitero di Praga*, Bompiani, 2010.

50   Cfr. Franz Hinkelammert, *Totalitarismo del mercado. El mercado capitalista como ser supremo,* México, 2018.

51   It was the thesis held by the U.S. Supreme Court in the late nineteenth century, cf. Morton Horowitz, *The Transformation of American Law. The Crisis of Legal Orthodoxy 1870–1960,* Oxford University Press, 1992.

52   This is how it is described in the *Encyclical Laudato si.*

superficially legal version with no further scope beyond measuring the effectiveness of laws according to econometric criteria.[53]

According to the henchmen of this ideology, any interference in the process of accumulation and concentration of wealth would only delay the future trickle, and if the state intervention that disturbs the market god is not contained, it will all end in totalitarianism, and it does not seem to matter if the cultural revolution is brought about by Keynes and Mao Tse Tung.[54]

Since all this trickling will take some time, an authoritarian and even totalitarian state is necessary in order to discipline those who do not yet enjoy the benefits of the trickle, and also to exercise a selective punitivity that does not disturb those who are accumulating wealth, even if their procedures are criminal. As can be seen, the structure of this thinking coincides perfectly with Stalinist thinking: until the *absolute good* is achieved (wealth trickles down to all) it is necessary not to disturb the accumulation of what will later trickle down. Hence, punitivity must be exercised selectively, in accordance with a *shameful* criminal law that guarantees accumulation for the rich and the containment of the poor, i.e. the people who *don't get it*.[55]

That is why the first Latin American experiment with this ideology was the Chilean Pinochet dictatorship, advised by Milton Friedman himself – the guru of the current – whose planners attributed freedom not to the human beings who lived there, but to the market. No wealth trickled down, but it did cost several thousand deaths by genocidal violence. This should not be surprising, because another evangelist of this idolatry maintains, in perfect opposition to all human rights, that the error consists in believing that every human being has rights just by virtue of being born.[56]

As financial capital monopolizes communication, it seeks to create a parallel reality, according to which those who do not receive any trickle-down should attribute that to the stereotypes of their own social class, *vagabonds* incapable of making the *meritocratic* efforts of those already deservedly enjoying their wealth, a blame that extends to corrupt politicians who advocate a minimally distributive state and who are stigmatized as communists or as vulgar thieves who seek only to meddle in public office.

---

53   We refer to the so-called *economic analysis of law.*

54   Friedrich August von Hayek, *Camino de Servidumbre*, Madrid, 2011, seems to express himself in this sense.

55   As von Hayek expressly says, they are simple people who are easily carried away by slogans.

56   Thus, expressly, Ludwig von Mises, *La mentalidad anticapitalista*, Madrid, 1995.

The prevailing nature of this power is the *creation of mediatic reality*, exercised through *media monopolies* or *oligopolies* (a Latin American original, since in no plural democracy is total deregulation of the media allowed), so that the same corporation or company can accumulate the ownership or concession of all television channels, radio waves, written newspapers and digital services.

Obviously, these monopolistic media become, sociologically, *political parties*, for they are the ones who select candidates aligned with the same financial power, who carry out their electoral campaigns, who defame those opposed to that power, and who launch the worst and dirtiest *fake news*, all with the old tactics of Goebbels,[57] unchanged save for the technology that, fortunately, was not available to him at the time.

In this way Latin American democracies are perverted, through the creation or invention of *unique realities*, into high-tech versions of the *Völkisches Beobachter* or *Pravda*. With modern technological resources, these *mediatic political parties* become unique parties who domesticate judges, lynching before public opinion those who are *indomitable*, and praising or publicizing the lies of those judicial minorities active in the arbitrary criminalization of political opponents, or in the criminalization of marginalized social groups.

If a government that does not respond to the interests of financial power takes any measure against these monopolies, it is deemed an attack on freedom of speech, when in truth, what really endangers freedom of speech is the very existence of these monopolies, incompatible on principle with any plural democracy. For that, they have the support of international organizations that look after their interests and their intangibility, especially favored by the deplorable conduct of the OAS General Secretariat in recent years, which expressly played to Trump's candidacy in the United States, intervened in the precipitation of the 2019 coup d'état in Bolivia,[58] and even interfered in the negotiations to resolve the conflict with Venezuela, postulating an armed intervention, that is, doing everything contrary to its manifest function as a continental organization.

This characteristic of transnational financial power and its local agents in our region has given rise to a completely new way of *dismembering* true criminal law: it glues the severed members together in a collage not by means of legal theory, but rather by its use of the media.

This is worth noting because it is something truly new in the history of criminal law. The previous versions of *shameful* criminal law (racist, Nazi, fascist,

---

57   Cfr. Gianluca Magi, *Goebbels, 11 tattiche di manipolazione oscura,* Prato, 2021.
58   Cfr. Evo Morales, *Volveremos y seremos millones,* Buenos Aires, 2020.

Stalinist, etc.) were *collages* which, on the basis of delusions, sought a certain internal discursive coherence that be invoked by their so-called judges. To discover their contradictions, it was necessary to dismantle the *shell* of legal rationalizations in which they were packaged, and which hid the ooze of the torn limbs and amputated trunk of *true* criminal law. But the legal debate, however deplorable it may have been, was maintained even at the academic level, theorized in the universities.

What is original about the current *shameful* criminal law is that it lacks not only this *shell*, but also any content to speak of. It elaborates itself in the field of marketing rather than that of law. The legal functionaries who want to use it thus have no choice but to adopt the rhetoric of advertising, since it is useless to look for legal arguments in the discourse of marketing technology. It is a question of publicizing arbitrary exercises of the function of judging merely by availing oneself of the media coverage offered by the communications monopoly. For this reason, the current *collages* do not even attain the base theoretical level of their predecessors, since they cannot surpass the level of discourse proper to mass media monopolies, in accordance with the well-known rule that the more irrational a power is, the more crass must be the level of discourse that pretends to legitimize it. In other words, there were Nazi, Soviet, Fascist and dangerous criminal law books that theorized these aberrations in criminal science, but there are no *lawfare criminal law books*, because in order to practice it, at most single sheets of paper are torn out of the current books, in accordance with what is arbitrarily decided in each case and circumstance.

9   The "Decapitated" Version of Today's "Shameful" Criminal Law

What is often termed *lawfare* in fact refers to the crimes committed by judges who exercise their power to criminalize popular politicians opposed to governments that respond to transnational financial interests, or to guarantee impunity for the local agents of those interests. These are sentences and other judicial decisions that in many cases fall into categories, since all penal codes penalize judges who fraudulently deviate from the law, either as a crime of prevarication, or as a particular form of the general figure of abuse of power against the administration. But even when those judges who proceed in accordance with one of the above-mentioned objectives do not fall into one of these criminal categories, they nevertheless walk on slippery slopes.

Consequently, now that the dismemberment of true criminal law in our region is no longer the work of jurists and their legal theories, it has passed into the hands of more or less explicitly prevaricating judges and the mercenaries of single media parties. Intervening as well are executive power officials, police agents (especially those in the secret or intelligence services), political operators, representatives of the executives in the judicial area, and other random characters, for this sort of criminal activity must be carried out by a relatively organized band or gang.

The judges who join these configurations and who skirt the edge of criminality, or swim within it, are not many, really a minority in each country. The vast majority remain silent and try to avoid being associated with these maneuvers. As we have said, while true criminal law is dismembered in order to fabricate *shameless collages*, there are also instances of the *decapitation* of *true* criminal law that facilitate the path of technocratic indifference. In the case of the persecutory *lawfare* wielded against popular political opponents, or used to protect the local agents of financial interests, the vast majority of judges take refuge in their bureaucratic peace or resort to *decapitation*, leaving it to the minority to compromise itself in such maneuvers.

But the silent majority, in addition to being functional by omission, since it does not obstruct the punitivity of the minority of judges who wage persecutory or cover-up *lawfare*, also renders an important service to the program, one that responds to the financial interests in the region. Often, the sensationalist protagonism of the compromised judicial minority makes us pay less attention to the consequences of the action of the silent and supposedly neutral majority of judges busy cultivating a *decapitated* criminal law, and we forget that they too tread on corpses, even as they feign themselves engrossed in syllogisms and idealistic speeches.

The social model put forward by the corrupt regimes of financial power's local agents tends to be configured with thirty percent of people included, and seventy percent excluded.[59] In order to control the growing number of excluded people, the exercise of punitivity becomes a necessity, not merely through excessive repression, as some believe, but rather through much more arbitrary, perverse and spectacular ways, so as to distract, confuse, and disconcert them.

To fulfill the functions required by the 30/70 social model, it suffices to apply just a modest degree of excessive punitivity against a small number of stereotyped, excluded subalterns. This creates the impression that the legal system is responding to the requirements of the *single media parties* who invented the

---

59   Cfr. Hans-Peter Martin/Harald Schumann, *Die Globalisierongsfalle,* Hamburg, 1996.

war on crime and the *general punitive populacherism,*[60] to later train them as thieves in prisons that have degenerated into concentration camps.

Once they are fully debilitated, humiliated, instilled with a deep social resentment, and assured of the impossibility of ever enjoying a productive life, these stereotyped and excluded people are released to go steal from their neighbors, in conformity with the direct relationship between poverty and risk of victimization. The same excluded and victimized groups then react by demanding a greater exercise of punitivity that, in the end, will end up being exercised only on them, thereby fomenting the fight of *poor against poor*. The state completes the cycle by sending out for their protection police workers without labor rights and who come from the same impoverished fringes of the population.[61]

Ever since the conquest, Latin America has known that the best colonization tactic is to generate conflicts between the groups to be dominated. With a very small number of soldiers, Hernán Cortés and Francisco Pizarro were nevertheless able to defeat the Aztecs and the Incas because they garnered the support of the Tlaxcalans in Mexico and the groups opposed to the Incas in Peru.[62] Dividing the people one wishes to conquer, making them fight among themselves and, if possible, making them ask for the dominator's help, is always an excellent control tactic, both internationally and internally.

For these reasons, the contributions – only seemingly of omission – made by supposedly *impartial* judges, refugees in the *decapitated* criminal law, are far from insubstantial. By contributing to the enterprise that allows the *poor to kill each other*, they prevent them from engaging in dialogue with one another or becoming aware of their situation. Any possibility of a coherent organization capable of resistance is therefore nipped in the bud.

We must keep in mind that all this is indispensable for the exclusionary social projects espoused by those transnational agents that influence our governments, and that vindictive or *punitive* discourse, besides being totalitarian and inhumane, is a weapon of electoral struggle that the local agents of financial interests always wield. The statement is clear enough:

---

60   A pejorative of populism: *"In short, it is nothing more than a variant or species of what is known by the old German term völkisch. Criminal populacherism is to ride on the worst discriminatory prejudices existing in a society and to deepen them in order to exploit them politically."* https://www.pensamientopenal.org/raul-zaffaroni-el-populacherismo-penal -es-una-tactica-detestable/.

61   Zaffaroni, Raúl, Alagia, Alejandro y Slokar, Alejandro (2002) *Derecho Penal. Parte general*, Buenos Aires: Ediar.

62   Cfr. Antonio Espino López, *La conquista de América. Una revisión crítica*, Barcelona, 2013; Tzvetan Todorov, *La conquista de América. El problema del otro*, México, 2009.

once an entire state is privatized, with multinationals that first use lob-byists to appoint ministers and then use the ministers to radicalize the privatization processes, democracy is already dead.[63]

We see, then, that the *neutral* and *aseptic* jurists, by remaining indifferent and allowing the cycle of punitivity against the stereotyped poor to continue, nec-essarily contribute to the program of colonialist social configuration reified by the regimes that respond to transnational financial power. It is not unusual for them to then present themselves as the *rightful* advocates of *decapitated* criminal law, and to cast all blame on the minority of judges who *dismembered* criminal law.

10   The Tendency of Dismembered "Shameful" Criminal Law to Sink to the Bottom

In theory, this sleight-of-hand selective punishment and its representation in the media, which renders punitivity impotent before the sidereal offenses of the local proxies of financial totalitarianism, as well before as the sensational-ist criminalization of their opponents, would dupe the public (supposedly *not very smart*) into believing that its most corrupt officials are in fact the only *pure and immaculate ones*.

But sometimes the crimes of local agents are too visible. In such cases, the use of unbridled punitivity against politicians adopts a new agenda, namely, that of instating so-called *anti-politics*, in which the public, always underesti-mated as fools, must be led to believe that all politicians are corrupt, resulting in widespread political apathy.

Now, this alternative method is always dangerous. It was the method used against plural democracy by the Nazis, who presented themselves as the move-ment that would overcome *partisan infighting*.[64] The risk of opening up this sort of system to a *maverick outsider* is notorious, as occurred with Alberto Fujimori in Peru, but the disseminators of *anti-politics* seem to be unaware of this, perhaps because they imagine that if a maverick outsider were to appear, he would ultimately play into their hands. However, it is also worth recalling that when Nazism and Fascism first emerged, many Europeans breathed a

---

63   Cfr. Vandana Shiva, *Fare pace con la terra*, Milano, 2012.
64   Cfr. Zaffaroni, *Doctrina penal nazi, La dogmática penal alemana entre 1933 y 1945*, Buenos Aires, 2017.

collective sigh of relief, believing they would halt the advance of socialism and communism.

In the rhetoric of anti-politics, corruption becomes the new *cosmic evil*, and politics the new Satan. His acolytes are the popular politicians (the witches of the moment), all of whom are inferior beings (witches being women), for only *inferior* beings would associate themselves with the *Evil One* (because inferior also means *corruptible*). Meanwhile, those who imprison their popular leaders and saddle their countries with astronomical levels of debt are *superior beings,* invulnerable to the temptations of the *Evil One.*[65]

It does not always happen, but from time to time, the local agents of global capital or their political associates let slip what they really think. In these moments of sincerity, they confirm their belief in the basic human inferiority of their political opponents, inferior because they are supported by the popular classes, by poor people of color, uneducated, ignorant, incapable of hard work according to the *meritocratic* criterion, and easy to deceive because, in general, they are backward *subhumans* who need to be supervised and tutored so that they do not get confused while voting and fall victim to *populism.*[66]

Throughout Latin America, the single-party media monopolies constantly promote, with thinly veiled racism, a visceral hatred or an internal anti-populist disposition,[67] trying to instill it in the middle classes – especially those who are not well established in that social stratum and suffer from a basic inferiority complex – and encouraging them to channel through this hatred all of their many frustrations.

These prejudices facilitate the mediatic modes of political persecution that exaggerate the alleged corruption of popular leaders to the level of a *cosmic* and *universal* evil. This institutionally pathological deformation of the law, whose arbitrariness is then disseminated by the single party media monopolies as further confirmation of its basic messaging, is *lawfare.* In the register

---

65   Cfr. *Malleus Maleficarum,* cit., pp. 315 y ss.

66   The expression *populism* in the "south" identifies popular movements which in the "north" would be considered left-wing or counter-left, but in the "north" it is used in a totally different sense, which is that of right-wing or völkisch populacherism. This confusion is exploited by the right wing of the "south" to impute "fascism" to them, which is absurd, because what characterizes the latter is an imperial component that can never occur in geopolitically subordinate countries. This has been recognized by European authors such as Eric Hobsbawn (*Historia del Siglo XX*, Buenos Aires, 2012, p. 121) and North American authors such as Michael Mann (*Fascists*, Cambridge University Press, 2004).

67   This *disposition* would be what in German is called *innere Gisinnung* and in Italian *attegiamento.*

of Shakespeare, both the minor players and the loftiest of the corrupt are alike appointed to the aforementioned mudhole of the judges.

While the lower and insecure middle classes are entertained by the circus-like spectacle of members of the legal world talking and writing nonsense, our supposedly incorruptible leaders take on debts in sums equivalent to years of GDP and then make millions of dollars of that debt disappear in the free outflow of capital. They make budgetary adjustments, repeal labor legislation, and defund scientific research, public health, and education. They privatize social security, sell off state patrimony at ridiculously devalued prices, and call for a *firm-hand* in punishing the delinquency of the stereotyped poor. These efforts to truly destroy states and pillage their economies have led *true* criminal law to consider the possibility of trying, at the international level, committers of *political economic crimes*, with the injured party being the economy of the entire population of a country.[68]

Because our current mode of *shameful* criminal law lacks any legal basis – for advertising only functions on the level of emotional impact, and does not aspire to reason – the minorities of the judicial world that have bowed to it now find themselves the orphans of a rational legal discourse. Perhaps for the first time in history, the *Satan* chosen is now so flimsy that any legal rationalization whatsoever will be adequate to the task of inquisition. The judicial minorities, who compound their general legal ignorance with a notorious lack of imagination, leave behind them at each step traces of new absurdities that, as a whole, begin to assume the form of a scandal.

The lead protagonists of persecutory and cover-up *lawfare* are judges who flirt with or commit the crime of prevarication or other forms of fraudulent activity. This creates some doubt as to the very meaning of *lawfare*. A compound of *law* and *warfare*, the term *lawfare* suggests a *warlike campaign of law* in the objective sense of the *law*, but is in reality nothing of the sort, simply because it is not legal, but criminal.

Leaving aside these merely terminological considerations, only relevant so that the term *lawfare* does not occlude its criminal nature, one must keep in mind that the active agents of lawfare are necessarily the judges; the other participants are instigators or accomplices. Consequently, we must delve a little deeper into judicial sociology, for not it is not just any judge who is willing to participate in borderline or truly criminal enterprises.

---

68   Cf. Wolfgang Naucke, *El concepto de delito económico-político. Una aproximación,* transl. and preliminary study by Eugenio Sarrabayrouse, Madrid, 2015.

This sociological parenthesis is indispensable because, as we have seen, it is always a minority of judges who actively participate in lawfare. The majority prefers to prudently take refuge in indifference, availing itself of the ostensible sterility of *decapitated* criminal law. What then are the motivations of the minority that chooses this tortuous path?

In principle, this deviation of conduct often results from long years of bureaucratic training, which tend to generate competitions for advancement in so-called *judicial careers*, a vice that is usually called *careerism* and that often leads to an excessive eagerness to jump supposed *judicial hierarchies* that, strictly speaking, are really nothing of the sort, since in the judicial field there are no hierarchies, just different specializations, because a judicial system is not a verticalized corporation, a fact not always understood in legal education. Since there would always be an incentive to defer to the designs of the political authority in charge of so-called promotions, judicial careerism may have some part to play in encouraging deviation from proper institutional conduct.

Institutional deformations aside, there are also individual factors such as the psychological disposition of the protagonists, for example inferiority complexes, possibly exacerbated by the perceived or real humiliations suffered in the line of duty, or by other traumas unrelated to their work as judges. Perhaps unconsciously they know that they do not exercise any real punitivity, but that by joining with the powerful of the moment, they too can feel powerful, and they *eroticize* their subjectivity with this *borrowed power*, without realizing that they will never really be *one of them*, since they are only used for as long as they prove useful.

In addition to these two factors, it is impossible to deny that there is always some glutton for publicity, some outlandish character dazzled by the lights of the television cameras that serve to boost his self-esteem before his social group and even his family. From time to time, some of these characters – only few, by the way, but it does happen – try to leverage their brief moment of television *fame* to enter into politics. These are the *star judges*. There are not many, and they are generally rejected by the other types of judges, who consider them a *contaminant* due to all their showboating.

The most notorious case is that of Judge Sergio Moro in Brazil, who, thanks to the absurd prosecution and preventive detention he imposed on Former President Lula da Silva (accused of having been gifted a property he never owned or held, for there was no documentation of delivery or acquisition), prevented da Silva from running for election and thereby made possible the victory of Jair Bolsonaro, who, once elected, made Moro his Minister of Justice and Public Security, until they butted heads and Moro was forced to resign. Moro's prevarication became fully apparent when Brazil's Supreme Court

THE DESTRUCTION OF CRIMINAL LAW

nullified all accusations made against the victim of this *lawfare scandal*,[69] a case of major political transcendence for all South America.

Those who seek fame usually end up looking ridiculous, and those who seek political power usually crash and burn. Very few succeed and even then, only for a short time, as was the case of Sergio Moro, who believed he would some-day succeed Bolsonaro himself thanks to the support of the single media party, which raised him to the summit of fame, only to then drop him vertiginously into the abyss. Because the judicial bureaucracy does not prepare them to play political games, the star judges are almost always guaranteed to fail.

Another factor that may incite a minority of judges to take the path of *law-fare* is one common to all crimes, namely the belief in one's impunity. For all the supposedly dissuasive power of punishment, we sometimes forget that criminals do not usually consult the penal code as if it were a list of prices on a restaurant menu. Moreover, the judges who opt for *lawfare* believe in their impunity because they assume that those in power will protect them, forget-ting that power is ephemeral.

In fact, the typical criminal act might be safer, because, knowing it has no power, it defaults to a defensive stance, while the kind of criminal we are dis-cussing here feels protected, insulated, and tends to overreact and leave too many traces. However, judicial lawfare has in its favor the precedent of a long history of unpunished judges, the most exemplary being the Nazi judges. Even the members of the political court itself (the *Volksgericht*) went unpunished, despite the atrocities they had committed. In Latin America, on the other hand, many of the judges complicit in the crimes against humanity perpetrated by the national security dictatorships of the 1970s have since been convicted.

11 The Consequences of *Lawfare*'s Dismemberment of Criminal Law

As we have seen, in Latin America *shameful* criminal law has no legal discourse capable of legitimizing the selective punishment of popular politicians, or of covering up the *macro-crimes* committed by the local agents of global financial power. The judges who choose this path are, doctrinarily speaking, exposed to the elements, their deliberations mere propaganda paid for by the single polit-ical party media monopolies. The decisions they make are utterly arbitrary,

---

69   Cfr. Luiz Inácio Lula da Silva, *A verdade venderá, O povo sabe por que me condenam,* São Paulo, 2018; Fernando Morais and others, *Vontade popular e democracia. Candidatura Lula?,* Bauru, 2018; Carol Proner and others, *Comentários a uma sentença anunciada. O processo Lula,* Bauru, 2017.

backed by the local agents of global financial power and covered by the media corporations.

Judicial resolutions and sentences do require some legal basis, some sort of argument. The Nazi, Fascist, Stalinist, and even National Security judges applied existing norms, however aberrant they might be, whereas Latin American *lawfare* consists of making decisions that contradict the very rules the judicial system has put in place, and which, at least from the point of view of *how things should be,* are not usually objectionable.

This endows *lawfare* decisions with a unique juridical – or rather, *anti-juridical* – quality, namely, that of resolving cases in direct violation of the law, without the protection or refuge of a legitimizing legal discourse. From a juridical perspective, then, the only way to describe the meaning of these decisions is through a continuous *dismemberment* of the true criminal law. That is, for each individual case, useful scraps of the law are reassembled, resulting in an infinitely varied series of *collages* of legal arguments, none of which have anything in common with the others.

The simple fact is that in lawfare cases the judges have already decided ahead of time to condemn (or protect) someone. They review the relevant legal volumes and tear out the pages they consider useful for rationalizing their decision. Often they cannot find any useful pages, even on the humblest pamphlet hidden away on the last shelf of the law library, and so they invent arguments that are not only inconsistent but also nonsensical.

Were an outside observer to stand back and contemplate the long series of prevarications, abuses of authority, and breaches of duties committed by the judges, their accomplices, and their instigators, she would believe that the rule of law has collapsed and that a bunch criminals now do as they please, simply because they can, justifying their actions with whatever they come across in a library or whatever comes into their heads, without the slightest consideration of legal precedents that have existed since the Romans, or of the doctrine established by the jurists of the present or the judges who preceded them. And of course they pay even less attention to constitutional texts. With the representatives of global financial power acting with impunity, their crimes covered up and those movements and parties who oppose them persecuted, one could very well conclude that in Latin America the rule of law is disappearing.

Of course, no rule of law has ever been perfect. The ideal model of the rule of law, under which everyone is equal before the law, has never existed. But it is useful to measure to what extent each historical rule of law deviates from the ideal. In comparison to the ideal model, the Latin American rule of law has always had some serious flaws, but at least, and with some twists and turns, the impulse to overcome its defects has also always remained alive. It now seems that *lawfare* has all but extinguished that impulse by means of a *shameful* criminal law that, dismembered by the actively corrupt minority and decapitated by the silent majority of judges, remains at the mercy of the political designs of the eventual and transitory agents of financial power.

12   Weaknesses Attributable to Legislators, Jurists, and Judges Outside of "Lawfare"

It cannot be denied that certain doctrinal, judicial, and legislative weaknesses may facilitate the assemblage of the incoherent *collages* of legal rationalizations discussed above. The science of criminal justice often forgets that it is necessary to sustain and continuously renew the spirit of the *founding fathers*. It has condoned or rationalized legal provisions and jurisprudential interpretations at odds with that spirit, making it easier for *lawfare* judges to find useful scraps for their *collages*.

It is impossible to review here all the flaws that were or are not officially recognized as antithetical to the spirit of the *founding fathers* or political liberals, and that provide fertile ground for nonsensical *lawfare* argument, but we can provide a few examples chosen at random from the Argentine legislation with which we are most familiar.

The most common of these provisions – and very useful to the minority of judges actively engaged in *lawfare* – is the type of conspiracy that, in Argentina, is defined in Article 210 of the Criminal Code, which punishes "whoever takes part in an association or gang that consists of three or more persons and whose purpose is to commit crimes simply by being members of the association."[70] Note that for the conduct to be considered criminal, they need only agree to commit a criminal act. That is to say, the simple fact that three persons agree to commit a crime is sufficient, and if a few minutes later they decide not to commit any crime, that decision would not even be relevant, because the criminal act would already have occurred, even without any legal property having been endangered. It should be mentioned that this type of criminal offense has a rather distasteful genealogy, as it was invented in Europe during the era in which it was a crime to go on strike, and for the purpose of criminalizing union leaders.

Obviously this is just a preparatory act, far removed from even beginning to execute the attempt. And yet the agreement itself can sometimes be punished

---

70   http://servicios.infoleg.gob.ar/infolegInternet/anexos/15000-19999/16546/texact.htm.

more severely than the crimes that were agreed upon: the penalty for agreeing to commit the crime is three to ten years in prison, but the offense itself may be theft, that is, shoplifting, which has a penalty of one month to two years. The constitutionality of this type of law is quite dubious, but it serves as grounds for denying releases from prison, as well as for convicting those who do not satisfy the requirements for being a perpetrator in cases of *delicta propria*, which are those crimes in which only those with certain specific characteristics (an official with jurisdiction, for example) can be perpetrators.

The small number of *lawfare* judges have not failed to exploit this possibility. For example, an official consulted by an autonomous organization regarding something over which he had no jurisdiction was convicted, and the only thing he did was to say that he was not qualified to decide. Because legally he was not the active subject, initially he could not be convicted, so an appeal was made in which they concocted his alleged involvement in conspiracy, all based on extremely flimsy evidence, and with the testimony of a *informant*, a *protected witness* who was paid with a hotel, that is, paid to hide, though all the while this supposedly *protected witness* was giving interviews to the mercenary friends of the local agents of financial power, interviews that were then broadcast on the television channels of the single party media monopoly. It is interesting to note that this case made it to the nation's Supreme Court, which decided it was not interested in hearing it, making use of its arbitrary power to refuse solicitations whenever it feels like it. This means that the Supreme Court of the Republic of Argentina finds it irrelevant that someone has been convicted on the basis of the testimony of a person paid to testify against him. But the invention of conspiracy has proven enormously advantageous for the political persecution of former officials, because it can always involve the head of power and even name her organizer or chief, rendering it possible to impose harsher punishment, and making for much more dramatic television.

Other devices that facilitate arbitrary convictions include treating preparatory acts as criminal acts, and the invention and cloning of legal assets so as to consider them independent entities. As a general rule, it is said that in these cases there is an *abstract danger*, an invention upon which legislators and doctrinarians converge and theorize with singular finesse, although with a certain naivety and ignorance of the most elementary principles of *true* criminal law. Danger – as reason and common sense point out – must be evaluated by the judge from the point of view he would have had before the incident (*ex-ante*), because after the incident the danger has passed. Therefore, the danger is always restricted to the incident. There is no normative, legal danger; the danger must have existed in real life. Legal doctrine departs not only from the law but also from common sense when it admits the possibility of an *abstract* danger that no one can identify and that it would be impossible to explain to a typical citizen. Danger must always be very *concrete*, really existing as a relevant possible result.

Some explain this oxymoron without renouncing the factual character of the danger and say that it is a *danger of danger*, which in cases of attempt would be a *danger of danger of danger*, that is, a very remote danger that, viewed from the perspective prior to the incident, was never a danger at all. The alternative would be to conclude that there is always a danger, but then that depends on the degree of paranoia of each observer, for there are always people who confuse risk with danger and recommend doing nothing at all because to them everything is dangerous. Fortunately, not all of these people are magistrates. Others forget the elementary principle that for a crime to have taken place, it must, by injury or endangerment, actually have affected a legal good, and, consequently, they ignore the factual nature of danger and admit that they are making a legal presumption of danger that admits no evidence to the contrary (a *juris et de jure* or absolute presumption), in other words, to save time, the law would take for granted that there is always a danger, even though it knows that in many cases there is not. Those who postulate an *abstract danger* in current Argentine law seem to forget that most of the world's legal systems include a constitutional principle that protects people's private actions from magisterial interference. This principle is translated into the so-called *harm* or *offense principle*, according to which there can be no crime if no harm – real, not invented by the legislator – has been done to another person's legal property.

Another widely used resource consists of confusing when a single act falls under several different categories or classes of crimes with the commission of several independent crimes. This happens frequently in jurisprudence, because the legal code is not always clear in this regard. Such confusion provides the perfect opportunity for *lawfare* judges to *replicate offenses*, no small matter, because instead of incurring the penalty for the most serious type of crime, in cases of several independent offenses, all penalties are added together. By this method a person can be acquitted of a crime, but then tried again for the same crime under a new label. One can then just continue going through the criminal code until the catalog of prosecutable offenses is exhausted.

Finally, there is no lack of imperfect or diffuse definitions of illegal conduct, multiplication of motives and evaluative elements, normative elements that are not very clear, etc. Examples abound. To mention only one, which certainly enables arbitrary action on the part of the police, recall that in Argentina, Article 237 prohibits any *intimidation or force against a public official*, but that Article 239 of the same code prohibits *resistance to authority*, without it being clear what *resistance* would be without intimidation or force. To top it off, the same Article 239 also declares it illegal to *disobey* an authority's order, as if every inhabitant of Argentina were obliged to comply with every order given by every official. In addition to all the above, there is the simple tactic – quite common and even considered ingenious, though it is usually nothing more than judicial vulgarity – of attempting to exhaust the prohibitive scope of the penal code with interpretations of a merely annotative or grammatical nature, with which insignificant effects on legal goods become crimes, or conduct protected by social convention becomes criminal.

Another resource used to prosecute political opponents is to impute them for results based on mere causation. If the civil servant's breach of duty seems too benign, then on an objective level, they accuse the civil servant of being responsible for consequences that could have been avoided by the omitted act, while on subjective one, they convert a possible negligence into an intentional effort to produce the result (*dolus* or intent). Admittedly, some parts of the legal code facilitate these feats of judicial legerdemain. But simple causality can never be a criterion of imputation, because causality is a chain of processes without beginning or end. As someone said long ago, a rape cannot be imputed to the carpenter who made the bed, any more than a given crime can be blamed on Adam and Eve or God himself for having created the world instead of leaving it all in chaos.

In short, and aside from the scandalous inventions of the small number of *lawfare* judges, there are many weaknesses in *true* criminal law itself that have nothing to do with persecutory or concealing procedures, but which nevertheless provide excellent materials for the prevaricators to construct their *collages*. Certainly, for the most part these weaknesses are not the result of malicious intent, but they are undoubtedly important doctrinal oversights, and the criminal justice system that has never attempted to delegitimize them or to challenge their notorious unconstitutionality cannot deny its share of the responsibility.

13   "Lawfare" Crimes

No Latin American is unaware of *lawfare* cases, nor of the scandalous persecutions committed by the agents of financial interests operating within the governments of the region, nor of the cover-ups, the impunities, and their maneuvers to overrun the state judiciary, but those who are not from our region and who are not familiar with these cases might be interested in considering some specific episodes of this sad series.

An exhaustive list is hardly possible, but as this is not a denunciation, it is only necessary to provide a few illustrations so as to give a more complete idea of *lawfare* prevarications and the ways in which judicial mechanisms are co-opted and neutralized, unbalancing the scale of republican justice. To this end, below are some examples, and though they have not been lifted word for word from real life, their resemblance to real cases is no coincidence.

1. A family company belonging to the president of a republic owes the state a debt of six million dollars. The company comes to an agreement with its creditors to pay one million dollars over an extended period of time. The contract is leonine (absolutely inadequate). An official in the public prosecutor's office objects and requests that the company be declared bankrupt and possibly fraudulent. She is denounced as a criminal and harassed at her home. Two people in her office then accuse her of abusive behavior in the workplace.

2. Supreme court judges must be appointed with the prior consent of the federal senate of a country. The president, without any precedent in one hundred and fifty years of the court's operation, decides to appoint two judges on an interim basis with no senatorial agreement. The proposed judges remain silent, that is to say, they tacitly declare their willingness to take office under these unconstitutional conditions. The legal scandal escalates. Finally the senate gives its consent and the two judges who agreed to the irregular appointment that did not materialize assume their roles and become the primary decision-makers as to the constitutionality of the nation's laws.

3. In the midst of the pandemic, the question arises as to whether children and adolescents should return to the classroom or continue with remote learning. One governor insists on the need to return to in-person learning in all schools. The federal government objects. The matter was taken to the supreme court, which did not summon any expert, despite the abundance of medical chairs and faculties in the country. The court, relying only on its own knowledge and belief, without any scientific argument whatsoever, rules that children must return to the classroom.

4. The former president of a republic is convicted of *a crime of instigation*. Every criminal law code in the world distinguishes between the perpetrator and the instigator, assigning them two perfectly separate roles, even in everyday life. The concept of a *crime of instigation* is absolutely incomprehensible.

5. A constitution, as a guarantee, defines treason against the nation, copying it from the Constitution of the United States, which establishes treason as a war-time offense, which consists "only in levying War against

[the US] or in adhering to [its] Enemies, giving them Aid and Comfort." This country has never been at war. And yet, with no war going on, a judge prosecutes high officials for *treason against the nation.*

6.   A court deems criminal a bilateral international treaty with another state that did not materialize because the counterpart did not ratify it, but which was ratified in its own country by both chambers of the legislative power. The executive branch officials are prosecuted, but not the senators or congresspersons, because it is presumed that they were *deceived.*

7.   Several officials of a previous government are prosecuted for alleged crimes for which there is only documentary evidence. Because of the sentence imposed, the officials have the right to continue the trial at liberty. However, this right is denied; the judge invents a presumption that every former official maintains *residual links* that may hinder the investigation, adding a grounds for non-release not codified in any law, and so the officials are kept in preventive detention. This means that any government official who is merely being prosecuted for a crime would not be entitled to release during the trial.

8.   A former minister who was undergoing cancer treatment in the United States is called to testify. The judge is informed of this circumstance and is asked to postpone the deposition for a very short time. The judge refuses and the former minister returns to his country so as not to be in contempt of court. The judge takes his statement and processes him, the processing delays his return to the United States to continue his treatment, and he dies.

9.   A judge calls a former president of the republic for questioning, and on the same morning he schedules the president for eleven separate hearings about eleven alleged independent crimes.

10.   The president of a republic strongly criticizes the traditional workers' party judges and lawyers, accusing them of forming a sort of illicit organization, and declares that he needs his *own judges*, because he cannot govern with these workers' party judges.

11.   A committee meets to decide whether or not a judge who is unfriendly to the executive should be impeached. One vote is needed to reject the request. A senator who was to join the committee that morning goes to the nation's supreme court to formally assume his duties. The chief justice of the court delays him for three hours, so that he can only join after the vote. They decide to impeach the judge by one vote.

12.   Flaunting precedents of every constitutional government, the president of a republic arranges for the transfer of judges between different

jurisdictions, thus filling the second-circuit courts with docile judges who exercise functions for which they did not have the prior agreement of the senate as required by the constitution.

13. A committee tasked with creating shortlists of candidates for judges summons the candidates, and the tribunals, regularly composed of specialists in the matter, issue their orders of preference. The plenary body, based on personal interviews, resolves to change the order of priorities, deviating from the practices previously established by the tribunals.

14. A provincial governor convenes his legislature, which resolves to increase the number of judges of the superior court. Two of the representatives who voted for that law resign their seats and are immediately appointed to the new vacancies that they created with their own votes.

15. An opposition leader of that same province is prosecuted for multiple offenses, or rather types of offenses via the tactic of replicating charges. The chief justice of the court declares that it would not be possible for the governor to govern if the accused were released. The chief justice (who is also the mother-in-law of the trial judge who prosecuted the opposition leader) resigns, another judge assumes the role of chief justice and declares the same thing. The opposition leader has been deprived of her liberty for more than four years, and is currently under house arrest by order of the Inter-American Court.

16. High officials are accused of having attempted to protect the perpetrators of a terrorist attack by trying to cancel the international warrants for their arrest. These warrants, issued by Interpol, can only be canceled by court order. The director of Interpol states that there was never any discussion of this alleged cancellation, quite the contrary, and offers himself as a witness. The judge closes the investigation without taking the director's testimony into account because he considers it unnecessary.

17. A judge summons a group of businessmen to testify. If they confess that they gave money to an official and they repent, he will release them, but if they do not confess, he will leave them in preventive detention.

18. A judge tries an official for receiving a payment, but dismisses the businessmen who admits having given the payment. These crimes always have two necessary participants, they are of necessary concurrence. The prosecutor does not appeal the decision.

19. The prosecutor who did not appeal this decision avails himself of his rights to not heed repeated summons to testify for participation in an alleged extortion. However, he continues to exercise his profession, remains active in all *lawfare* trials, and intends to build a case against the judge who summoned him for questioning.

20.   An attorney general with decades of impeccable service is threatened.
       She is accused of having benefited from a small sum of money in the
       purchase of a building. Her daughters are called to testify. She had pre-
       viously been warned that if she did not resign, she and her family would
       be harassed. Her daughters' telephone numbers were made public. She
       received all kinds of threatening messages. She finally resigned, and was
       still prosecuted.

21.   A coup d'état takes place. The president and the vice-president are
       forced to evacuate in a foreign military plane that can barely leave the
       ground. During take-off, they are fired upon by a missile that misses its
       target. While in exile, the country calls an election and the president
       registers as a candidate for senator. His candidacy is rejected because
       he is not residing in the national territory.

22.   During another coup d'état in the region, the police open fire on dem-
       onstrators, leaving forty people dead. The government of a neighboring
       country immediately provides military supplies to the de facto regime
       in a manner completely inconsistent with its own legislation. Thus far
       no one has been arrested, despite detailed documentary proof of the
       delivery of the smuggled materials.

23.   A supreme court grants the release of persons convicted of genocide
       by twisting the interpretation of a law. A scandal ensues, a million peo-
       ple gather to protest, and the legislature passes an *interpretative* law
       that prevents the court's criteria from being applied in the future. The
       judicial majority of the supreme court decides to change its ruling, but
       instead of expressing it in this way, they state that they accept that there
       are supposedly *interpretative* criminal laws, with which they do nothing
       more than retroactively apply a harsher penalty, an act expressly forbid-
       den by the constitution, which prohibits the retroactive application of
       laws unless it serves to benefit the defendant with a lesser sentence.

Again, that these examples coincide with reality is no coincidence. We believe
these instances sufficiently demonstrate the magnitude of the judicial institutional pathology thus far discussed, and the serious way in which they endan-
ger democratic and republican models in Latin America.

14   Would it Not Be Prudent to Prevent "Lawfare"?

Everything changes, nothing is static, Heraclitus was right. *True criminal law* is
dismembered but then recomposed, for even when it loses its way, in the end
the human being always wants to be free. Regrettably, dismembered law often

leaves corpses in its tortuous wake. But we must avoid going to the extreme of jettisoning the law as a useless tool – a dull knife or a hammer without a handle – because then only violence will remain, and the corpses will all belong to the most disadvantaged, who lose even if they eventually triumph, because human lives cannot be recovered.

But we cannot conclude our dizzying overview of the destruction of *true criminal law* without observing some of the contradictions proper to the popular politicians themselves, today persecuted by the mechanisms of the new *shameful criminal law*. It is not a question of accusing them of anything; we are well aware that politics in our region is a constant combat on too many fronts. It is not our intention to blame the victims, but we cannot fail to formulate a warning for the future, to point out to them that in their own administrations, either out of naivete or in order to win or retain votes, too many times they neglected *true* criminal law, they condoned the passing of absurd laws, they gutted criminal codes, they adopted vindictive rhetoric or yielded to it, they let themselves be intimidated by the campaigns of single parties mass media monopolies and of unscrupulous politicians, and they selected judges who were known to practice a *decapitated* or worse, *shameful* criminal law.

A good part of those judges who today make up the judicial minority of docile prevaricators were appointed or promoted by popular governments, and many of the absurd laws now used to persecute politicians in our region were enacted with their signatures. We would encourage them to be more careful in the future.

CHAPTER 2

The Destruction of Law of Criminal Procedure

Cristina Caamaño

1   The Impact of the Political Media Usage of Law of Criminal Procedure in Argentina

In recent years, a kind of *freezing of constitutional guarantees* has occurred in Latin America, led by a certain judicial sector.[1] A minority sector, it is true, but with substantial support from mass media hegemonies, faithfully adherent to a political agenda whose sole purpose is to persecute national and popular governments. This phenomenon is widespread and clearly evident in many countries, but in our region it has become increasingly dramatic. In Brazil,[2] Argentina,[3] Colombia, Bolivia, Venezuela and other countries,[4] *constitutional freezing* is the ground floor of a very complex architecture of judicial perversion and distortion. As we stated in the introduction, the traditional principles of Law of criminal procedure, closely linked to the subject's constitutional protection from punitivity, are the primary safeguards frozen:[5] the presumption of innocence, legality, impartiality of the judiciary, double jeopardy,

---

1   Santos, Roberto Santana; Pitilllo, João Claudio Platenik; Villamar, María del Carmen [orgs.] *América Latina en la encrucijada: guerra de leyes*, golpes de Estado y lucha de clases. Trad. Roberto Santana Santos y María del Carmen Villarreal Villamar. São Paulo: Autonomia Literária, 2020.

2   Zanin Martins, Cristiano; Zanin Martins, Valeska; Valim, Rafael [coords.] *El caso Lula*: la lucha por la afirmación de los derechos fundamentales en Brasil. São Paulo: Contracorrente, 2016.

3   Bielsa, Rafael y Peretti, Pedro (2019) *Lawfare. Guerra judicial-mediática. Desde el Primer Centenario hasta Cristina Fernández de Kirchner*, Buenos Aires: Planeta.

4   Romano, Silvina M. (comp.). *Lawfare: guerra judicial y neoliberalismo en América Latina.* Buenos Aires: Mármol Izquierdo Editores, 2019.

5   In addition to the principles in the strict sense, a characteristic of the vulgarization of the criminal procedural process is the extremely problematic insertion of civil procedural categories into the criminal process, such as the ill-fated "relative nullities," which permit any illegality practiced by judges, police and prosecutors in the criminal process to be overlooked, or the construction of "conditions of action" totally alien to the theory of the criminal process, among others. On this, see, for example, Lopes JR. Fundamentos del proceso penal: introducción crítica. 6th ed. São Paulo: Saraiva, 2020; Coutinho, Jacinto Miranda. The life and content of the criminal process. Curitiba: Juruá, 1989; Silveira, Marco Aurélio Nunes da. *Por uma teoria da ação processual penal.* Mentalidad acusadora, vol. 1. Observatorio de la mentalidad inquisitorial.

exceptionality and the extraordinary nature of coercive measures, all of which, in *lawfare*, are reduced to absolute zero. It is necessary to calmly analyze the concrete procedures of criminal law to understand how this freezing of the constitution is directly leading, step by step, towards its destruction.

The mechanism always operates the same way: a shocking headline – possibly fake news – is introduced into public opinion. A childish belief in the "magical powers" of punitivity to solve conflicts then propagates itself in the collective imagination:

> In an unequal society, subjected for more than four centuries to a state of marginalization and social exclusion, in which primitive knowledge is mixed with that of the dominant power and becomes an instrument of simple survival, the belief in punishment as a resource capable of symbolizing the destruction of evil becomes widely spread and deeply fixed. In this context, the belief in punitivity is not the product of the free and rational choice of free citizens, but rather the natural consequence of the oppressive processes internalized in society and one that further contributes to inequality and authoritarianism. Paulo Freire observes that, in the formation of intersubjectivity, the oppressor will always manifest the tendency to mystify reality so that the oppressed grasp it as fixed and therefore accept it as a natural phenomenon. The mystification of reality solidifies the internalization of oppressive procedures. [...] Adherence to the criminalizing norm, therefore, is associated not only with tradition, but also with the capitalist process of transforming people themselves into commodities and sedimenting the belief in the need to eliminate expired products.[6]

The mechanism of fake news had already been denounced by Perseu Abramo in Brazil, who notes that citizens believe, faithfully and rigidly, that this fake news is really a part of the truth, and that in fact it reflects "public opinion." Fake news necessarily contains absolutely negative words ("corruption," "embezzlement," and "fraud" are very useful).[7] "Political party X stole millions!"

---

6   Tavares, Juárez. *Crimen: creencia y realidad*. Río de Janeiro: Da Vinci Livros, 2021. pp.130–131.
7   The delegitimizing discourse of the Workers' Party (PT) in the 2018 elections in Brazil was essentially cast as a conflict between "the corrupt *versus* the non-corrupt." This proposition was put forward in absolutely false terms, as pointed out by Davi Tangerino, professor at the State University of Rio de Janeiro. The creation of this narrative was indispensable for the election of the extreme right-wing government that took over the country from that moment on, but it had no factual basis. Empirical figures show neither that the Workers' Party was the "most corrupt" – quite the opposite – nor that the opposition

"The former president was quoted in the *End of the World Whistleblower* by Whistleblower Y!" "A conversation between X and Y was leaked, in which they discussed bribes and kickbacks and corruption and diabolical plans and the atomic bomb and the end of the world!" This "news" is then disseminated by the media hegemonies, regardless of whether or not it has any factual basis or the faintest resemblance to a reality[8] that could render it anything more than the sensationalist rhetoric of newspaper anchors, "influencers," and "content creators."

Meanwhile, in the judicial sphere, criminal proceedings are initiated and only then does the collection of evidentiary material[9] begin. It is irrelevant if they are photocopies that can never be examined[10] or that do not provide evidence,[11] or if it is not possible to explain how the evidence was

---

candidate, Jair Bolsonaro, was the "most probative – also quite the opposite." This demonstrates the essential role of the creation of *parallel realities* in the dynamics of today's pseudo-democracies. See Tangerino's indispensable and lucid analysis at <https://www.youtube.com/watch?v=rlwkkPHZGyk>. Accessed on: 10/11/2021.

8   For the reader who is not accustomed to legal language, we offer a simple explanation: the concrete exercise of punitivity must always be supported by a reality that supports it, that serves as its foundation. This is so for the simple reason that this type of exercise of political power, an expression of the sovereignty of a state, is the most drastic intervention in the sphere of a person's fundamental rights. Such an interference, whose practical consequence is *punishment*, whether public or resulting from informal social control, can never be based on speculation, unrealities, or illusions.

9   The practice of gathering evidence after having already taken a position is called *fishing for evidence*. It is an "indiscriminate speculative investigation, without a determined or declared objective, that 'casts its nets' in the hope of 'fishing' for any evidence that will support a future prosecution. [...] If the first step of 'going fishing' is to mask the illegality of the investigative procedures, the next step is the attempt to legitimize the act. Thus, just as it happens in a fishing expedition when the fishermen catch some fish and gather to take a picture and show the catch, it also happens in the evidentiary expedition of the criminal proceeding." Ghizoni Silva, Viviani; Melo E Silva, Philipe Benoni; Morais Da Rosa, Alexandre. *Expedición de pesca y encuentro fortuito en búsqueda y captura*. Florianópolis: EMais, 2019. *Apud* Morais Da Rosa, Alexandre. *La práctica del fishing expedition en el proceso penal*. jul./2021. Available at: <https://www.conjur.com.br/2021-jul-02/limite-penal-pratica-fishing-expedition-processo-penal>. Accessed on: 10/11/2021.

10   On the importance of the *chain of custody of evidence* for a democratic and constitutionally grounded criminal procedure, see Prado, Geraldo. *La cadena de custodia de la prueba en el proceso penal*. 1st ed. Buenos Aires: Marcial Pons, 2019.

11   Argentine judge Claudio Bonadio – to whom we will return shortly – ordered the imposition of *numerous judicial measures* against former Argentine President Cristina Fernández de Kirchner in the so-called "Notebooks Case" based only on photocopies of supposedly original manuscripts that would have been destroyed. Lorenzo, Martín Fernandez. *Ditadura togada*: el extraño pedido de detención de Cristina Kirchner en Argentina. sep./2018. Available at: <https://www.socialistamorena.com.br/ditadura-togada-o-bizarro-pedido-de-prisao-de-cristina-kirchner-na-argentina/>. Accessed on: 10/11/2021.

obtained,[12] when it took place, or what the details are.[13] The goal is to sell political news, which society buys without questioning it (since if it appears in the media it has to be true), but the most important thing of all is to annihilate the political opponent. That is to say, using Law of criminal procedure as a tool, a new aim is sought, namely, the political death of those who oppose the sector that defends the most powerful economic groups.[14] This objective has no correlation whatsoever with the fundamental ideal of building a procedural system of rules able to check the power of the state and protect its citizens against the arbitrariness of official power.

This phenomenon, which some years ago was termed *lawfare*, has the immediate and direct effect of weakening democracy and of consolidating a political-media government that leaves its citizens vulnerable to the whims of global powers and large economic groups. As we saw in the previous chapter, the main characteristic of this form of abuse is the use of criminal law and, in particular, the attribution of a new role to Law of criminal procedure, which now becomes a weapon in a "struggle" that should be strictly political. "Fights," "battles" and the like are categories proper to politics, and more specifically to

---

12   Former Brazilian judge Sergio Moro defended in 2016 the validity of using illicit evidence in criminal proceedings, as long as it had been obtained "in good faith." Cf. at <https://www .conjur.com.br/2016-ago-05/moro-defende-uso-prova-ilicita-teste-integridade-servidor>. Accessed on: 10/11/2021. For a more specific critique of this "legal argument," see Streck, Lenio Luiz. *Illegal evidence validated by good faith*: there goes the kid with the dirty water. aug./2016. Available at: <https://www.conjur.com.br/2016-ago-08/prova-ilicita-valid ada-boa-fe-la-bebe-agua-suja>. Accessed on: 10/11/2021. An interesting detail is that the defense of this position was made when the public debate on the famous "10 measures against corruption" in the Brazilian Parliament. This occurred despite the fact that at that time Moro was still a federal judge and the Brazilian Constitution expressly prohibits, in a clear and inflexible manner, a magistrate from engaging in political activities (art. 95, III, CF).

13   Freitas, Janio de. *Moro condenó a Lula por "acto indeterminado del cargo," es decir, inexistente*. Enero de 2018. aveilable at: < https://www1.folha.uol.com.br/colunas/janiodefrei tas/2018/01/1952105-moro-condenou-lula-por-ato-de-oficio-indeterminado-ou-seja-nao -existente.shtml>. date of accessl: 30/11/2021.

14   On the importance of discourses and media news involving precautionary detentions, criminal cases and trials, as well as the various functions that all this plays before public opinion (establishment of paradigms, stigmatization, normalization of ways of acting and thinking, dissemination of symbolisms, promotion of "public sanctions") see Cunha, Luana Magalhães de Araújo. *El destino producido por la noticia: la muerte estampada en los periódicos*. Belo Horizonte: Editora D'Plácido, 2019; Cunha, Luana Magalhães de Araújo. Notícias da prisão: justiça e vingança no enquadramento jornalístico das prisões de natureza cautelar. Belo Horizonte: Editorial D'Plácido, 2019. Cf. also Batista, Nilo. *Medios de comunicación y sistema penal en el capitalismo tardío*. Available at: <http://www.bocc .ubi.pt/pag/batista-nilo-midia-sistema-penal.pdf>. Accessed on: 30/11/2021.

wartime politics. They have no place in law.[15] All this unfolds while preserving a certain *aesthetic of democratic institutionality*, since the maintenance of this facade is essential for reaffirming the "sanctity" of the discourse while hiding its ideology.

Now, why is the judiciary being used to conduct political battles? Perhaps because it is the only branch of government whose members are not directly elected by the people? Or is it the idea that the judiciary embodies a *technical* power, not a *political* one?[16] The answer may vary depending on our interpretations of reality and, for this reason, we will limit ourselves to extending throughout these pages an analysis of different instruments that will question the naturalization of the use of a constitutional tool such as Law of criminal procedure into something totally contrary to republican principles, which destroys it by transforming it into *shameful law of criminal procedure* (we follow here the concepts defined in the previous chapter).

We have seen, then, that this whole phenomenon of lawfare is something like an undeclared war.[17] In this war, the deviant use of criminal procedural criminal law acquires various characteristics: it alters the rules of competence and jurisdiction, violating due process; it arbitrarily manipulates the figure of the "informant;" it makes use of illegal wiretapping and abuses preventive detention in cases that clearly and evidently do not deserve the imposition of this precautionary measure. All this clearly heralds the end of criminal law as

---

15   If we place ourselves in the Ferrajolian perspective that law should aspire to be an instrument to achieve peace, we have here, in the concept of *lawfare*, as previous literature has already pointed out, the just antithesis of law: *war*.

16   On the "de-ideologized judge," see Jacinto Nelson de Miranda, Coutinho. *El papel del nuevo Juez en el proceso penal* Apr./2015. Available at: <https://emporiododireito.com.br /leitura/o-papel-do-novo-juiz-no-processo-penal>. Accessed on: 11/11/2021. In contrast, on the importance of the judge recognizing his specific political-legal commitment to the emancipation of people through the protection and enforcement of the Constitution and fundamental rights, see the interesting Souza, Artur César de. *La "parcialidad positiva" del juez y el justo proceso penal:* nueva lectura del principio de (im)parcialidad del juez frente al paradigma de la "racionalidad del otro." Doctoral thesis. Graduate Program in Law of the Legal and Social Sciences Department of the Federal University of Paraná – PPGD-UFPR. Curitiba, 2005. Available at: <https://acervodigital.ufpr.br/bitstream/han dle/1884/3046/R%20-%20T%20-%20ARTUR%20CESAR%20DE%20SOUZA.pdf?seque nce=1&isAllowed=y>. Accessed on: 11/11/2021.

17   This war is not authorized by the National Congress in a typical constitutional act, public and debated, as required, for example, by art. 49, II, of the Brazilian Constitution, which establishes in favor of the Congress the competence to authorize the President of the Republic to declare war, which must also be done by an express and declared act, as provided by art. 84, XIX, of the same Charter. *Lawfare* is, therefore, a furtive war, a war that is not assumed and that is fought under the regulatory cloak of war.

an instrument for containing the insatiable punitivity of the state[18] and ushers in its *anti-democratic* function. We are going to unveil these common practices, all part of what we might call, as previously mentioned, *shameful Law of criminal procedure*.

It is enough to consult recent jurisprudence in Latin America to see these legal tricks at work. The first of these, which is central to the others, involves a circumvention of the guarantee of due process. While trying a criminal case, for example, it may happen that other criminal acts appear that were not included in the initial investigative scope of the accusation; this forces the opening of new judicial proceedings, which do not necessarily have to be carried out by the same judicial body.[19] For this purpose, there is a series of twists and turns that must be sufficiently transparent to make it look as if *forum shopping*[20] is not taking place. However, within the framework of lawfare, it somehow "magically" happens that the cases against certain political opponents always fall to the same judge (and even prosecutor); and if this does not happen, in all likelihood some situation will force jurisdiction to fall to the judge who can best carry out the political attack on the opponent.

A key tool in these processes is the figure of the "informant." Of dubious constitutional soundness, this figure derives from the fact that a defendant may offer evidence to obtain ill-gotten assets, or to incriminate another defendant with greater responsibility in the act and to receive in exchange a reduced sentence. To prevent defendants from inventing accusations for their own personal benefit, the use of a informant's testimony is only appropriate when the information he provides truly serves to clarify the fact; that is, it must be corroborated and confirmed by other evidence in the case file or investigation.[21] His statements alone are not enough.

---

18   In fact, this is the only possible function that Law of criminal procedure, a complex and intricate system of logical, argumentative, legal and political rules and norms, should have in a democracy.

19   See, for example, the decision of the Brazilian Supreme Court in Investigation No. 4,130.

20   It is a common term to designate the behavior of one of the parties in a litigation proceeding to force a non-existent or incorrect jurisdiction of any court. In short, it is the conscious and directed choice of the jurisdiction most favorable to the interests of one of the parties.

21   For example, in Brazil, Law 12.850/13, article 4, paragraph 16, establishes that measures such as sentencing, personal or real precautionary measures and the receipt of indictments or charges cannot be based exclusively on elements from an informant's complaint. These provisions, introduced into domestic law by Law 13.964/19, certainly represent some progress in terms of criminal legislation, but the courts still do not apply it.

However, this is not what happens in lawfare cases; on the contrary, the informant enjoys a nominally reduced sentence and, as a consequence, is released from prison, while the judge is now authorized to incriminate other persons, effectively those political enemies previously targeted for legal persecution, regardless of whether or not they are linked to the event that gave rise to the initial investigation. That is to say, the figure of the Informant is not used to provide more information or clarify a controversial fact (as established in the Constitution), but rather to incriminate those whom the judiciary wishes to annihilate.

Another element at the disposal of the judge is wiretapping, as we have seen in the first chapter. It is an extremely coercive measure[22] that is used both inside and outside of criminal trials.[23] Here the dual irresponsibility shared by the judiciary and the media is elemental to the success of the endeavor. It is irrelevant whether the audio produced during wiretapping really clarifies a criminal act or whether it simply offers the media an opportunity to humiliate those who cannot defend themselves by legal means.

In Argentina, the wiretapping system depends on the Supreme Court of the Nation; once again, the judiciary gains ground in the struggle for power because now it not only judges, it also investigates, a practice that flies in the face of the accusatory system, whose theoretical core is the separation of the functions of judging and accusing, a principle meant to impose a minimum level of restraint on punitivity. Through the control of wiretapping, the judiciary is responsible for judging, investigating, directing the criminal process, and guaranteeing respect for our privacy in telecommunications. And yet it has repeatedly leaked to the media audio recordings that have nothing to do with the accusations made in the case for which they were ordered.

Equally unconstitutional is the use of pretrial detention for cases in which, based on objective premises, there is no danger of flight or of hindering the investigation, these being the only admissible reasons for the state to deprive a person of his freedom when he has not yet been convicted. However, this is one of the primary tools used to eliminate anyone even mildly oppositional from the political map. It does not matter whether there is a danger of flight or of obstruction of the investigation; nor does the quality of the evidence collected in the case matter, nor whether a provisional release is appropriate for the crime. What really matters is the annihilation of political opponents.

---

22   See principle of *subsidiarity* or *exceptionality*.

23   Eventually, the interception may be determined when a formal process based on a formal complaint has not yet been initiated, i.e. in the course of preliminary investigations, police inquiries or similar activities of the criminalizing agencies.

In short, we must not lose sight of the fact that when people are given erroneous information (fake news), even if it is later disproved or cannot be proven in the framework of a lawsuit, it causes irreparable damage. The media monopoly, of course, desires this effect, and finds support from the judicial body in the form of courtroom proceedings. These are the basic ingredients of lawfare.

2   Jurisdiction and Due Process

To make sense of the following pages, we must first address some basic principles. In this section we will define and describe our key concepts and then, once all the cards are on the table, we will present our arguments on the subject.

Jurisdiction is the power to act that the law attributes to a public official. In this context, we are primarily concerned with the jurisdiction granted to those who intervene in criminal cases.

Jurisdiction has specific characteristics: it is non-extendable, meaning the parties cannot petition that the matter be resolved by any judge other than the one to whom it corresponds; in other words, jurisdiction cannot be manipulated according to the desires of the interested parties. Jurisdiction is also non-delegable, meaning judges cannot transfer their functions to other officials. Nor can jurisdiction be refused by those involved in the case, i.e., the plaintiff and defendant cannot choose their judge any more than the judge can deny his jurisdiction and the consequent responsibility to try a case or a person, except in situations in which he perceives a specific impediment[24] or suspicious circumstances.[25] And finally, jurisdiction in criminal proceedings is a public charge, i.e., it is not at the disposal of private interests. In sum, the rules of jurisdiction are established in the constitution and in laws and regulations, according to criteria such as time, territory, result, subject matter and hierarchy, for the purposes of delimiting when and how a given official may intervene in a criminal case.

The concept of due process, meanwhile, is part of the block of guarantees that protects all citizens when the state, within any of its spheres of influence (national, provincial, or municipal), exercises its jurisdictional powers and, consequently, discharges its punitivity through officials of the judiciary or the public prosecutor's office. Thus, the guarantee of due process is summarized in the phrase that states that "no inhabitant of the Nation may be tried by

---

24   For example, when one is a relative of the accused.

25   Cases in which their impartiality may be tainted generally occur in situations of extreme political enmity or divergence.

special commissions nor be denied trial under the judges appointed by law before the fact of the case," as established in the Argentine Constitution as well as in the constitutions of the rest of the continent and the world. This is one of the fundamental criminal procedural guarantees, since it protects a person from being subjected to a jurisdiction that is exceptional, interested, or one that lacks constitutional and legal validity. Moreover, due process is also a public guarantee of a transindividual order. Its benefits transcend even individual defendants because it acts as a safeguard that permits society as a whole to trust its jurisdictional system. Additionally, the guarantee of due process helps prevent the executive branch from using the judiciary as a political weapon, for example by replacing judges prematurely, changing the jurisdiction of its courts, or forming new or special courts to the detriment of the criminally prosecuted. In other words, in addition to an individual guarantee of justice, the criminal procedural principle of due process is an organic institutional prerogative, essential to the very independence of the judiciary.

This legal principle is so important that it was enshrined in the American Convention on Human Rights, better known as the Pact of San José, Costa Rica, which codified it under the heading of *Judicial Guarantees* as one of the fundamental pillars on which the entire system of human rights protection is built. This treaty has constitutional status in Argentina and many other countries of the region (in Brazil, given some jurisprudential particularities, its constitutional or infra-constitutional character is still being debated).[26]

It should be clarified that, although in this chapter we refer to the guarantee of due process including a judge with jurisdiction in criminal matters, with the passage of time and, fortunately, a more dynamic and broad interpretation of constitutional principles, constitutional guarantees have come to apply to all judicial processes or administrative procedures carried out by the state.[27]

---

26   Under severe criticism from the specialized literature, the Federal Supreme Court in Brazil has upheld the supra-legal character (above ordinary legislation and below the Federal Constitution) of the Pact of San José (STF, RE 466.343). This position is not the most compatible with international law for the protection of human rights. Even from a legal-dogmatic point of view, it is clear that each and every treaty whose object is the protection of human rights, for this reason alone, already has a materially constitutional character, regardless of the procedural forms by which the convention was internalized in domestic law. This distinction has practical relevance, such as the submission of ordinary legislation, before treaties, to an effective control of constitutionality.

27   In this sense, one can consult, for example, the IACHR Case González et al. v. Mexico in 2019; the IACHR Case Nadege Dorzema et al. v. Dominican Republic; and the IACHR Case Jesús Vélez Loor v. Panama. The Court also ruled similarly in the Ivcher Bronstein v. Peru Case and the Constitutional Tribunal v. Peru Case.

Having explained the origin of the principle, let us now define the concepts that compose it. In every legislative system on the continent, the figure of the judge has specific requirements. In Argentina, the judge is a citizen who, after passing a competitive examination and having been appointed by the executive body, is designated by the Congress of the Nation to hold office in any of the judicial branches or courts with criminal jurisdiction. The same procedure is to be followed when appointing prosecutors and public defenders, two other relevant figures in all criminal proceedings. The procedure for the investiture of judges may differ somewhat from nation to nation: in some countries, judges are subject to a public election process, while in others, depending on the position within the jurisdictional hierarchy, they are compatible with appointments without requiring a public vote.[28] The concept of "natural" then derives from the judge's exercise of his or her function, whether he or she is the head of a court charged with investigating the commission of a punishable act, or a member of a court that convicts or acquits the person tried for such an act. What is important is that it is only through legislation and the constitution that the judge is granted jurisdiction to act in a particular case.

In this sense, it should be clear that, as citizens, we are not guaranteed the right to be judged under the same procedural regime or by the same judge until the end of the case, as the rules of procedure and competence are of public order and thus liable to change, especially when they regulate the way crimes are investigated and their perpetrators prosecuted. Additionally, judges, who are people and not demigods, may retire or be promoted. In other words, the guarantee of due process has nothing to do with granting benefits or privileges to anyone: on the contrary, its whole purpose is to prevent the privilege of exception. One of the first institutionalizations of this postulate is to be found in the former Article 17 of Title II of the French Law of August 24th, 1790, which stipulates that "the constitutional order of jurisdictions may not be disturbed, nor jurisdictions subtracted from the appropriate judges, by any commission, nor by other assignments or evocations." The only exception was provided for "cases determined by law." In other words, the legal system establishes the jurisdiction of public officials, be they judges, prosecutors, police, or public defenders.[29] Jurisdiction must not be influenced by the personal or vested interests of these officials or by those of other bodies.

---

28   For a comparative study on judicial organization in various countries of the world, see, Gonçalves, Gláucio Ferreira Maciel; Andrade, Érico [coord.] La *organización judicial en el derecho comparado*: Alemania, España, Estados Unidos de América, Francia, Gran Bretaña, Italia y Portugal. Río de Janeiro: Lumen Juris, 2018.

29   According to the most current literature and the requirements of the Inter-American Court of Human Rights, the principle of due process applies to each and every public

What international treaties and their laws do not tolerate, regardless of whether they have constitutional or supra-legal hierarchy, is that a citizen or a criminal case under investigation by a judge be removed from his jurisdiction by unconventional means and tried by a new magistrate whose ultimate goal is to harm or favor the accused. Nor is it permissible to create special courts to try specific individuals or cases at specific times.

Having clarified these concepts, we begin our analysis. The concept of due process was conceived (or at least written) in a context in which the criminal procedure model was eminently inquisitorial. The competent judge in charge of a case conducted the investigation, assessed the evidence he himself had gathered, and handed down the sentence. He was, as he is today, a very powerful subject. Wisely, then, the requirements for occupying the position were made more stringent in order to prevent the government of the day from only placing judges who would favor their personal interests. As we have said, the figure of due process serves, among other things, to guarantee the independence of the judiciary, and ultimately, of democracy itself.[30]

In the countries that follow the Grecoroman tradition, the entire criminal-legal structure of the judicial system was designed with the inquisitorial process and the central role of the judge in mind. The procedural codes, which regulate issues of jurisdiction and competence, make this clearly evident. For example, prosecutors have the duty to ensure the legality of the trial and to promote and encourage criminal prosecution, but there is still the possibility of an examining magistrate.[31] Fortunately, the paradigm is changing, and the procedural systems are leaving aside the examining magistrate, an obviously paradoxical figure that *shameless Law of criminal procedure* has been quick to exploit. Indeed, *true Law of criminal procedure*, through reforms and the

official who exercises functions in the course of criminal prosecution, and his or her powers must be previously established in legislation and in the Constitution. This is because the public official represents the state as a whole, and the state can only act impartially and with interventions authorized by the legal system.

30   See, for example, in the European Court of Human Rights, *the case of Pozharskyi v. Estonia.*

31   Brazil has a robust inquisitorial tradition that persists unchallenged by most intellectuals, producing harmful effects in judicial practice. Only very recently, with Law 13.964/19, did the legislature insert verbatim in the Code of Criminal Procedure the prohibition for the judge to substitute the prosecution to substitute his rulings. Even so, the device encounters great resistance in the literature and in a huge sector of jurisprudence. Gloeckner, Ricardo Jacobsen, *Autoritarismo* (op. cit.); El Tasse, Adel. *¿Qué es la impunidad?* Curitiba: Juruá, 2009; Duclerc, Elmir. *¿Garantismo penal integral o defensivismo dietético?* Available at: <https://1library.org/document/qogkk4jz-garantismo-penal-integral-ou-defensivismo-diet.html>. Accessed on: 30/11/2021; El Tasse, Adel. *¿Qué es la impunidad?*. Curitiba: Juruá, 2009.

application of new rules, has progressively abandoned the inquisitorial model in favor of an accusatory (or at least more accusatory) one. In other words, the cards have been shuffled and new roles have been assigned to the actors in accordance with the Constitution: for there to be a legitimate criminal process, the judge must be impartial, both subjectively and objectively,[32] and for this reason, the judge should not be involved in collecting evidence,[33] lest he become both judge and plaintiff or defendant and influence the outcome of the trial with personal biases of which, many times, he is not even aware.[34] This is prohibited by our Constitution, but it continues to happen today for two reasons: because there is legal support for the delay in reforming the procedural code at the federal level (much of the new code sanctioned in 2014 has yet to be implemented), and because of judicial and political interests in ensuring that certain magistrates retain the power to direct investigations.

Why are the names of the judges that appear in the news almost always the same? Why do these judges often decide to involve themselves in the investigation of cases, even though this is in direct conflict with constitutional principles? Why do they decide not to delegate investigations to prosecutors when they have the option to do so?

The concentration of power has been engorging itself since the 1990s. The judiciary and legislature have engendered that legal monstrosity known as the Examining Magistrate, who is at the same time both judge and interested party, and who participates not only in the judicial process, but also in political strategies shaped or consolidated through practices in which he gathers papers, evidence, and pseudo-evidence for the purposes of achieving objectives outlined in boardrooms far removed from the halls of justice.

---

32   European Court of Human Rights (ECHR), *Piersack v. Belgium*; Inter-American Court of Human Rights (IACHR), *Apitz Barbera v. Venezuela.*

33   European Court of Human Rights (ECtHR), *Cubber v. Belgium,* as well as *Hauschildt v. Denmark.*

34   In the field of neurobiology, there is an incredible range of empirical and scientific studies on confirmatory biases, moral judgments and stigmatization based on poverty, skin color and previously constructed emotions about a given subject. Sapolsky, Robert. *Compórtate: la biología humana en su mejor y peor momento.* Trad. Pedro Pacheco. Capitán Swing. Madrid, 2018. On the innumerable factors affecting the decision-making process, it is also interesting to read the award-winning Kahneman, Daniel; Sibony, Olivier; Sunstein, Cass R. *Noise: a flaw in human judgment.*

3   The Difficult Road to Judicial Impartiality

We believe that one of the first steps to repelling this monster is to implement the intended normative change of *true Law of criminal procedure*; recall that the legislator, as well as the judges, plays a fundamental role both in destroying and in reconstructing Law of criminal procedure. A change must be made that prevents judges from exercising investigative or prosecutorial function, and that removes criminal policy decisions and the direction of the investigation from the hands of an omnipotent magistrate who violates the guarantee of impartiality and therefore the citizen's constitutional rights, since he invades homes, seizes personal documents, and arrests whomever he pleases with no authority beyond that which he derives from his political backers and his own pen.

Once this is achieved, we then need prosecutors with firm convictions, who remain independent and detached from politics. (Members of the executive branch should not be nominating their friends, relatives or highschool buddies for these positions, while for their part, the political connections and self-promotional agendas of the prosecutors are often blatantly obvious.)[35] It will not be an easy equation to solve, nor will it be simple to eliminate judicial vices that have for centuries been deeply rooted in the theory and practice of inquisitorial criminal procedure. Those who wield real power will, within their massive zone of influence, make use of new weapons and rules of jurisdiction in order to influence prosecutors to conform to their interests and to exert pressure on those who do not. With the normative banishment of the figure of the examining magistrate, we must also ensure that prosecutors are not surreptitiously co-opted as Trojan Horses for the purposes of criminally prosecuting the same people as always or of undermining the basic tenets of a republic by subjecting criminal law to private interests.

4   The Informant

The question of the partiality of judges and prosecutors, and the problems related to the systematic violation of the guarantee of due process are, as we have seen, central to lawfare, but they are certainly not the only problems that *shameful Law of criminal procedure* poses for us. There is a figure in our legal

---

35   In Brazil, not only the judge in the case against Lula (Lava-Jato) decided to go into politics, but also the prosecutor responsible for the indictment.

system that, in recent years, has appeared with some frequency on the front pages of newspapers and in various television and radio news programs, where he has made an enormous impact: he is that mass media character known as the "informant." The political utility of this character in the news and on social networks has in recent years earned him a great deal of attention,[36] but this phenomenon is neither new nor recent; references to the Informant date back to ancient Greece, and he appears in Roman Law and in the Napoleonic Code of 1810.[37]

In Argentine law, the Informant first appeared in 1950, in Law 13.985, which incorporated the crimes of espionage and sabotage into the Criminal Code. The figure was subsequently included in criminal and criminal procedural legislation on several occasions: in 1994, Law 24.424 was enacted, which amended Law 23.737; in 2000, Law 25.241 on "Acts of Terrorism" and, in 2003, Law 25.742, which incorporated Article 41 into the Criminal Code. Finally, during the neoliberal government of former President Mauricio Macri, who governed from 2015 to 2019, Law 27.304 was enacted for cases of corruption, drug trafficking, and human trafficking, among other crimes. This law modified article 41 of the Criminal Code, and gave a more prominent place to the figure of the "informant."

The law includes two very distinct structures: it reduces the penalty of the accused in exchange for information that serves to clarify a punishable act already committed; and it reduces the gravity of the crime for the perpetrator or participant who, with his help, prevented the initiation, continuation or consummation of a crime. Well, if we are talking about preventing the beginning of the execution of a crime, we are undoubtedly referring to the acts that precede it, i.e., the preparatory acts. This already poses a legal problem. There is a large body of doctrine and jurisprudence pointing to the legal impossibility of punishing preparatory acts;[38] acts that precede the perpetration of an offense are exempt from criminal liability.[39]

---

36   See, for example, the interview granted by Geraldo Prado, one of the greatest Brazilian criminal proceduralists, at: <https://www.redebrasilatual.com.br/revistas/2018/09/a-midia-as-delacoes-e-a-contaminacao-do-sistema-de-justica/>. Date of access: 21/11/2021.

37   For a study on the "prolonged reality in the history of criminal law" of the subject, cf. e.g., Dalbora, José Luis Guzmán. Del premio de la felonía en la historia jurídica y el derecho penal contemporáneo. In: *Revista de derecho penal y criminología*. 3ª Época. N. 7 (January 2012). pp. 175–196. Available at: <http://revistas.uned.es/index.php/RDPC/article/view/24604/19497>. Date of access: 03/11/2021.

38   Zaffaroni, Eugenio Raúl; Pierangelli, José Henrique. *La tentativa: doctrina y jurisprudencia*. 3a ed. rev. e atual. São Paulo: Editora Revista dos Tribunais, 1992.

39   The provision of these "punitive barriers" is one of the central characteristics of what has come to be known as *the criminal law of the enemy*.

Moreover, in order for the benefit to be granted, the information provided by the accused must, by law, help "to avoid or prevent the initiation, continuation or consummation of a crime," as well as serve to clarify the circumstances of the crime (perpetrators, exhibits, etc.). In other words, the contribution must be significant and corroborated by the other stages of the investigative proper to *true criminal procedure law*. On its own, it is of no use, it is mere hearsay, and must be considered insufficient to convict a person or to make judicial decrees that act to his detriment, such as precautionary detentions, telephone interceptions, and so on. All this derives from the principle of the presumption of innocence.

Of course, the information provided by the informant may very well be accurate, verifiable and reliable. However, if the investigative steps are not carried out efficiently and safely, the information may lose its relevance, e.g. due to the passage of time, which turns the cooperation of the accused into the loss of a "great opportunity" for the prosecution. In this case, the cooperating person took a great risk completely in vain, without any benefit, in circumstances now entirely irrelevant to him.

Another possibility is that the information provided by the supposedly informant person is completely false and only an attempt to improve his legal situation, something we have observed very often in Argentina and its neighboring countries.[40] Indeed this happens so frequently that one wonders whether this law simply serves to introduce lies. Through the use of falsehoods, any truths created become part of *shameful Law of criminal procedure* and thus the judiciary contributes to the imposition of a distorted reality.

5 The *Magical Realism* of the Informant

And so it began to rain Arcadios in Macondo, as if we were living in a magical realist novel by Gabriel García Márquez.[41] If by cooperating a defendant can obtain his freedom, he is likely to invent all sorts of stories that might benefit him. This has happened and continues to happen in the current judicial system in Argentina, as well as in Brazil, where criminal prosecution agencies have made an extortive use of pretrial detention (which we will go into in more detail later), turning it into a bargaining chip to obtain confessions from

---

40   Cf. Morais Da Rosa, Alexandre. *Para entender la delación premiada por la teoría de los juegos*: tácticas y estrategias del negocio jurídico. Imprenta: Florianópolis, Modara, 2018.

41   García Márquez, Gabriel. *Cien años de soledad*. Ed Sudamericana, Buenos Aires, 1999.

the accused in order to incriminate political enemies.[42] The operation is very simple: the preventive imprisonment of a defendant under investigation for a crime is ordered so that, upon interrogation, he "confesses" and provides information about the crimes he committed and the other people who participated in them (it does not matter if it is true). In this way he can regain, at least for a little while, his freedom. This is an authoritarian and inquisitorial absurdity, but it happens very often.[43]

Now, what is the reward for this "repentance?" If the information provided by the accused is corroborated by other evidence, Argentine law imposes that the informant will receive a reduction of one third of the maximum and one half of the minimum sentence. Unlike its Brazilian counterpart, under no circumstances does this law allow for the penalty to be altogether eliminated.[44] But the punishment, in both cases, is used as a bargaining chip, as an asset in the negotiation. This is completely incompatible with the supposedly resocializing purpose of punishment. Punishment itself loses all justification when it is diminished and transformed into a kind of functional reward that is given or denied by the justice administration as part of a political power play.

What is more, there may be cases in which, based only on circumstantial convenience provided by the informant innocent people are convicted. In this way, as the Italian jurist Luigi Ferrajoli has pointed out in many of his works, the system of guarantees in the criminal process is put at risk; but of course this does not matter in the context of *shameful Law of criminal procedure*. It is necessary to look for a good number of "informants" who not only expose the crimes allegedly committed, but also deliver a few banalities that serve to portray certain people as undesirable and representative of every evil besetting the nation.

---

42   In Brazil there is even a type of pretrial detention designed exclusively for this purpose. A vestige of authoritarianism – which, despite having been enacted in a law subsequent to the 1988 Democratic Constitution, was inspired by the times of the military dictatorship in the country – is temporary custody, which consists of segregation for a set period of time during the course of a police investigation. According to the relevant legislation (Law 7.960/89), it is applicable when the deprivation of liberty is essential for investigations. In practice, however, it is an extortion measure used as investigative torture to obtain a confession from the accused.

43   https://noticias.uol.com.br/politica/ultimas-noticias/2019/10/02/gilmar-lava-jato-usou -prisoes-provisorias-como-instrumento-de-tortura.htm>. date of access: 01/12/2021.

44   In Brazil, the legal schemes and benefits of collaboration agreements are mostly found in Art. 3 – A of Law 12.850/13, including the possibility of a sentence reduction of up to 2/3, the substitution of deprivation of liberty for the restriction of other rights and judicial pardon, among others.

6   The Systematic Violation of Constitutional Guarantees

As stated in Article 18 of the Argentine National Constitution, and in analogous versions in the nation's other fundamental charters, "no one is obliged to testify against himself." To say that the author or participant of a crime "voluntarily" admits the fact and that this does not affect the above-mentioned guarantee is a fallacy as the article forbids it. It is possible that the accused, by acknowledging his participation in the crime and providing other information, runs the risk of a more severe punishment, seriously undermining the constitutional guarantee by encouraging self-incrimination.

Another principle affected by this figure of the informant is that of equality before the law. In Argentina, Article 16 of the Argentine National Constitution provides this guarantee, as do Article 24 of the American Convention on Human Rights and all other international documents for the protection of human rights in the world. The sanction imposed on the Informant is influenced by his behavior throughout the trial, while those who did not have special information about the act in which they participated tend to receive unequal and discriminatory treatment. This can occur, for example, in criminal organizations dedicated to drug trafficking, where there are different hierarchical levels of participants and each of them has different degrees of information about the criminal activities involved. Indeed, in large organizations, those with less hierarchical power tend to have less information about the general dynamics of potentially criminal activities, while the leaders are not only better informed, but also the ones who coordinate these activities. This means that the head of a criminal organization, even if he coordinates and directs the group's activities, may be much less affected by a criminal prosecution than a hierarchical subordinate would be, since the former possesses a great deal of relevant information with which to negotiate. Thus, the "boss" may secure more benefits (despite his greater responsibility), while those on the lowest rungs will serve a longer prison sentence (despite their lesser responsibility). Finally, one person may be punished more severely than another for the same act depending on the information he or she possesses or does not possess, thus affecting the principle of equality before the law, which in the context of criminal justice can be defined as the principle by which each person is answerable according to his or her participation in the crime, and to the extent of his or her own guilt.

Similarly, those arrested first will have an advantage over others who may be arrested later. If they wish to, and if they reach an agreement with the prosecution, the first accused will have access to the benefits derived from the information they can provide. They may even be able to remain at liberty while participating in the trial. This situation gives the prosecution an enormous amount of power, since it allows them to deliberately choose with whom they want to make these agreements, and to direct the investigation with an eye towards benefitting certain people rather than obtaining useful information. In this sense, during their preliminary hearings, those arrested later will have much less of a chance of reaching an agreement with the prosecution, since the first detainees will have already provided the most relevant information.

Finally, the figure of the Informant also violates the principle of culpability, by which a person can only be punished to the extent of his or her acts. This violation is clear in the provisions of Article 41 in the Argentine penal code, which provide for a reduction of the penalty for those who "cooperate," so that the penalty imposed is directly affected by the conduct of the subject during the trial. That is to say, the penalty will no longer be linked to the individual's culpability for the act perpetrated, but rather to his or her willingness to cooperate with the prosecutors.

7   Lies Instead of Proof

The nature of the figure of the informant is simply that of a pact. The legislators are not at all interested in whether the perpetrator or the participant of the act truly repents. Their aim, instead, is to encourage the exchange of information that may help, to a greater or lesser extent, the investigation of a crime, in exchange for a benefit in the form of a reduced sentence or the granting of freedom during the trial. Sincere repentance has nothing to do with seeking such benefits. The fabrication of truth does not even pose a major problem for *shameful Law of criminal procedure* as long as it can insist that the truths it presents to us are irrefutable.

Thus, although the Dictionary of the Royal Spanish Academy defines repentance (*arrepentimiento*) in terms of the conduct manifested by the accused in acts intended to diminish or repair the damage of a crime or to facilitate its punishment, this definition is not exactly coherent with what we have been analyzing. When repenting, the accused is expected to "confess his sins," as a Catholic believer confesses in the Sacrament of Reconciliation. The Brazilian jurist Nilo Batista points out that this sort of "conceptual promiscuity between crime and sin" sacralizes the one and politicizes the other. It speaks not to the culpability or innocence of the accused, but rather to his or her morality, translating the confession into a "politically correct" and virtuous act.[45] To use the terms laid out in the previous chapter, in the face of a *cosmic evil*, religion and politics join forces, but without necessarily defining that evil as strictly criminal. In fact, they take the criminal process and milk it for all it's worth: what matters is that the "sinner" exposes the other personifications of evil. As Thomas Hobbes once argued: "A crime is a sin consisting in the committing by deed or word of that which the law forbiddeth, or the omission of what it hath commanded. So that every crime is a sin; but not every sin a crime."[46] Terms such as repentance, denunciation, and collaboration are then invoked in an effort to take actions colloquially known as "snitching," and behaviors and personal characteristics historically considered unethical, disloyal, or immoral, and make them appear positive and ethically virtuous. But the euphemism has only succeeded in exposing the failures of the criminal system, and the incorporation of the figure of the informant into our legislation has paved the way for countless instances of *shameful Law of criminal procedure*. This type of figure merely permits the institutional manipulation of those under investigation, as we have seen in the federal courts, and due to the abuses of pre-trial detention, freedom has become the bargaining chip for these so-called informants: "cooperate, my brother, and you will be free, but first tell me: who is the Evil One?"

Fighting corruption and other complex crimes using information gleaned from "confessions" likely obtained under duress has no value, legally or morally. The offer of a reward or benefit presupposes the possibility that the accused may invent, exaggerate, or simply acknowledge his participation in an act simply out of fear of receiving a heavier sentence, so that his freedom of action is undoubtedly attenuated – more so if he is being held in pretrial detention. The unregulated use of the figure of the Informant by some judges and prosecutors has made the federal courts the central and most important venues for political extortion, since they endorse judicial decisions based on falsehoods, thereby affecting the freedom of individuals and permitting the persecution of political opponents.

45   Batista, Nilo. *Matriz ...* (*op. cit.*). p. 163.
46   Hobbes, Thomas. *Leviathan.* https://liberalarts.austincc.edu/philosophy-religion-humanities/chapter-27/.

THE DESTRUCTION OF LAW OF CRIMINAL PROCEDURE

8   Wiretapping and Other Coercive Measures of *Shameful Law of Criminal Procedure*

So far we have seen some of the diverse procedural ramifications of *shameful criminal law*'s distortion of the guarantees to which any person accused of a crime is entitled. Nor is the *shameful law of criminal procedure* limited to a concentration of cases in a single court, the "denaturalization" of *due process* or the use of the figure of the informant. It also makes public the most private conversations and communications: a person's dialogues with his family, his colleagues, and even his trusted lawyer, all for the purpose of convincing the public that the accused is the archetype of a despicable, horrible, corrupt, and, above all, vulnerable person.

One might point out that this is not the objective of the criminal process. Of course it is not, but that does not matter to the *shameful law of criminal procedure*, which now devotes itself not to the collection of evidence of criminal activity, but rather to the political persecution of opponents. This exercise of Law of criminal procedure works solely to identify and locate targets for trial and public scorn.

There is a shared consensus among constitutionalists regarding the inviolability of epistolary correspondence and telephone communications. In fact, a systematic reading of the provisions of fundamental rights establishes equivalent protection for all these aspects of the private and intimate life of citizens. Constitutional protection seeks to grant a zone of immunity, exempt from the authority of the courts, to those spheres in which the "private actions" of individuals normally and predominantly take place.[47] This "shielding" is one of constitutional criminal procedure's basic conditions for a civil society.[48]

---

47   In Brazil, the constitutional protection of privacy is contained for the most part in Article 5, points x and xii of the Federal Constitution.

48   This view is supported by the case law of the German Constitutional Court. "The German Constitutional Court, when examining the unconstitutionality of the constitutional amendment to Article 13 of the Basic Law [...] qualified several articles of the Code of Criminal Procedure as unconstitutional. This is so because, as that Court stated, "the inviolability of the home is closely related to human dignity and to the constitutional requirement of unconditional respect for an exclusively private – 'strictly personal' – sphere of development. Confidential communication requires a spatial protection on which citizens can rely. The individual must be guaranteed the right to be alone, especially in his private space, without fear that the state authorities will monitor the development of his personality in the central sphere of private life (Decision of 03/03/2004)." Tavares, Juarez; Casara, Rubens. *The evidence and the truth*. 1st ed. São Paulo: Tirant lo Blanch, 2020. pp. 70–71.

The regulation of the guarantees of privacy reasonably allows for a court order to execute a coercive measure, always under reservation of jurisdiction, that is to say, in this matter the judge has the first and final say. The magnitude of the intrusion into constitutionally protected situations and spheres of life resulting from the determination of an interception of communications requires a careful consideration of its necessity, and a concrete justification at the time it is ordered. The interception of communications is one of the most coercive measures in criminal proceedings, even more drastic than a house search, due to its possible duration and the number of people affected. Not only do we listen to an individual, but also to his family, his lawyer, and even to the delivery boy.

Moreover, these communications are filed away for access by the court and the parties involved in the case, and are not destroyed, even when it becomes clear that they contain no information that can be considered evidence of a crime. Not infrequently, they are also leaked to the media, filling hours of screen time or newspaper pages, to once again remind the public that the accused is a despicable, horrible, and corrupt human being.

9   Wiretapping

Every story has a beginning and someone who tells it. The story we will tell is that of a long journey, with many dark episodes, and so we will touch only on its most significant milestones. In Argentina, many years ago, the interception of communications effectively depended on the state-owned company ENTEL, although all the people in that sector were intelligence agents. Years later, after the privatization of ENTEL, the sector responsible for the interception of communications was integrated into what was then called the State Secretariat of Information. However, the company continued to administrate all "eavesdropping" activities. (It is worth clarifying that, from the beginning, the functions of this interception sector, regulated by a secret "S" decree, were very broad, and it was the "competent authority," i.e. the judge, who ordered these interceptions.)[49] Then came a succession of (many) more secret decrees issued by

---

49   On the privatization of ENTEL in Argentina, see http://www.laizquier-dadiario.com /Privatizacion-de-Entel-historia-balance-y-lecciones, http://www.enorsai.com.ar/polit ica/10693-his¬torico--maria-julia-condenada-por-la-privatizacion-de-. On the contrary, the web page of ICCSI (Iniciativa Ciudadana para el Control de los Servicios de Inteligencia) reflects all the proposals and discussions tending to build a democratic agenda around the intelligence services: https://www.iccsi.com.ar/.

the military dictatorship that ruled the country between 1976 and 1982. One of them was Decree "S" 416/76, which changed the name of the Secretariat of State Information to the Secretariat of Intelligence (*Secretaría de Inteligencia del Estado*, SIDE).

When the privatization of ENTEL made it impossible to restrain the activities of this sector (perhaps the Spanish, Italian and French telecommunications investors did not want intelligence agents snooping around their offices), the National Executive Power issued Decree No. 1801/92, which transferred the interception sector to the SIDE. In 2004, Law 25.873 was passed, which modified an earlier regulation that had diminished telephone service providers' role in the interception of communications in favor of the judiciary or the Public Prosecutor's Office. Ever since, the private telephone companies that replaced ENTEL (Telecom and Telefónica) have been the ones who do the telephone tapping, collecting the personal data of all their users and keeping these records on file for ten years in case a judicial authority requests them. This practice was questioned in the Ernesto Halabi[50] case heard by the Supreme Court of Justice of Argentina in 2009.[51]

Nevertheless, the arbitrary use of wiretapping has continued. After years of serious questions regarding the discretion of intelligence operators in their use and filtration of wiretapping, National Intelligence Law 25.520 was enacted, which, in addition to assigning the operation of the Judicial Control Directorate (known as the DO) to the Secretariat of State Intelligence (the SI, formerly the SIDE), attempted to modify the use of these interception procedures, for the purpose of ensuring that they could only be carried out with judicial authorization.

This law, however, perpetuated the old ambiguity between intelligence activity and criminal investigation. As has been pointed out by several

---

50   Ernesto Halabi, an Argentine lawyer, filed an order of protection against the state, declaring the unconstitutionality of Articles 1 and 2 of Law 25.873, and its regulatory decree 1.563/04. The regulatory decree he challenged incorporated three provisions to the National Telecommunications Law (Law 19.798): firstly, that telephone companies intercept communications requested by the Judicial Power and the Public Prosecutor's Office, secondly, that such telephone records had to be archived for ten years, and thirdly, that the state was responsible for the eventual damages that this measure could cause. The plaintiff filed his complaints alleging that his rights to privacy as a user and as a professional were violated, as was his ability to maintain confidentiality in his communications with his clients.

51   http://www.saij.gob.ar/corte-suprema-justicia-nacion-federal-ciudad-autonoma-bue nos-aires-halabi-ernesto-pen-ley-25783-dto-1563-04-amparo-ley-16986-fa09000006 -2009-02-24/123456789-600-0009-00ts-eupmocsollaf .date of access: 02/12/2021.

representations and denunciations of the Citizens' Initiative for the Control of the Intelligence System (*Iniciativa Ciudadana para el Control del Sistema de Inteligencia*, ICCSI), this law meant that the interceptions considered matters of intelligence (and therefore requiring a judicial order) belonged to the same physical and factual powers as the interceptions ordered by judges in the context of open criminal proceedings. In other words, the confusion between the two types of wiretapping (those of the intelligence agencies and those of the courts) stemmed from the institutional location of the Judicial Observations (*Observaciones Judiciales*, OJ) in the SI, as the only body competent to carry out the interception of communications.

Hours, days, and years of illegitimate relations between a considerable sector of the federal justice system and intelligence operators has led to the continuous leaking of wiretaps of private and political conversations, whose darkest and most complex moment was the death of the federal prosecutor Natalio Alberto Nisman, discussed below. In an attempt to check this problem, then-President Cristina Fernández de Kirchner decided to intervene in the operations of the SI and, in 2015, Law 27,126 established the Federal Intelligence Agency (*Agencia Federal de Inteligencia*, AFI).[52]

This law also transferred to the Attorney General's Office the OJ and its delegations, and determined that it would be the only state body responsible for interceptions or any kind of seizure authorized or ordered by the appropriate judicial authority. This transfer consecrated the role of interception as a strategic criminal investigation tool exclusive to *true criminal law* (both material and procedural).

Motivated by this transfer, the Attorney General's Office, then headed by Alejandra Gils Carbó, created the General Directorate of Investigations and Technological Support for Criminal Investigation (*Dirección General de Investigaciones y Apoyo Tecnológico a la Investigación Criminal*, DATIP) and incorporated the former OJ into the Department of Interception and Capture of Communications (DICOM). Thus, DICOM became the only state body with the power to intercept or capture any type of communications, authorized or ordered by the appropriate judicial authority, i.e., those ordered by the officiating judge or by the prosecutor in the cases provided by law (in particular, the investigation of crimes of extortion by kidnapping or illegal deprivation of liberty). Although the interception of communications was the responsibility of the Attorney General, not only were the interception procedures, commonly

---

52   http://servicios.infoleg.gob.ar/infolegInternet/anexos/240000-244999/243821/norma
      .htm.

known as "wiretapping," transparent and quick, but, more importantly, they were not leaked to the media. At that point there was no room for *shameful criminal law*. The spaces that did exist were duly limited so that there were no gaps or loopholes.

10   The Eavesdropping Continues

Elected president in 2015, Mauricio Macri, after publicly expressing his enmity with Gils Carbó, ordered, as one of his first actions in office, the Decree of Necessity and Urgency 256/15 (dated December 24, 2015).[53] By means of this decree, the interception of communications was transferred back to the Supreme Court, circumventing the parliamentary procedures required by a decision of such magnitude, and disregarding the obvious fact that the highest jurisdictional authority, i.e. the judges responsible for determining the reasonableness and legality of "wiretaps," cannot also be in charge of executing these measures. This immediately ushered in a new stage of *shameful criminal law*.[54]

After assuming this task, the Court expanded the functions of this sector of interception of communications and created the Directorate of Judicial Assistance in Complex Crimes and Organized Crime of the judiciary (*Dirección de Asistencia Judicial en Delitos Complejos y Crimen Organizado del Poder Judicial de la Nación*, DAJUDECO), whose mission was to assist judicial authorities in complex cases of organized crime. It is obvious that the expanded powers granted to DAJUDECO encroached on the competencies of the Public Prosecutor's Office, the only body with the constitutional right to perform these tasks. The Court also delegated the function to a federal magistrate appointed by a supposed lottery, though his assignment had already

---

53   http://servicios.infoleg.gob.ar/infolegInternet/anexos/255000-259999/257346/norma
      .htm.
54   On the leaks of private wiretapping in Argentina, see: https://www.pagina12.com.ar
      /103358-la-corte-pidio-investigar-las-filtraciones, https://www.infonews.com/politica
      /majul-problemas-la-difusion-escuchas-cristina-y-parrilli-n270538, https://www.cij.gov.ar
      /nota-29618-La-Corte-Suprema-pide-que-se-investiguen-las-filtraciones-de-escuchas
      -telef-nicas,html; https://www.ambito.com/edicion-impresa/corte-suprema/corte
      -murmura-culpa-filtraciones-escuchas-la-afi-y-jueces-federales-n5035574, https://www
      .perfil.com/noticias/politica/aseguran-que-ya-no-quedan-espias-a-cargo-de-las-escu
      chas.phtml, http://www.laizquierdadiario.com/Un-ano-de-mentiras-de-Clarin-y-La-Nac
      ion-sobre-Santiago-Maldonado. https://realpolitik.com.ar/nota/29432/caso maldonadoh
      ubounafiltraciondeaudiosmuyselectivafuncionalalateoriadelgobierno/.

appeared in the mainstream media days earlier. Of course, one may wonder what the investigation of complex cases of organized crime has to do with the private conversation of a person with his family, friends and trusted lawyer. Well, nothing.

11   The Unconstitutional Interception of Communications

Notwithstanding the significant constitutional problems raised by the formation of the DAJUDECO, which seriously compromise the principle of impartiality, the fact is that ever since wiretapping was transferred to the Supreme Court, there has been a constant flow of information leaks in which clearly private communications that would have no relevance in the context of *true Law of criminal procedure* are broadcast on television and published in newspapers and magazines.

In short, a brutal and incessant disclosure of private conversations have been put on public display. And thus an investigative tool, one proper to *true Law of criminal procedure* and which should be used only in an exceptional and reasonable manner since it violates fundamental rights, becomes a weapon wielded by state agencies for the purpose of shaping and altering public opinion, that is to say, a weapon at the service of *shameful Law of criminal procedure.*

Now, the word "leak" is fairly benevolent in situations of obvious and vulgar revelations of information and conversations that took place within the most intimate spheres of people's lives. However, without lingering on merely terminological issues, it is worth remembering that the seriousness of these *leaks* was such that the Supreme Court itself ordered both Congress and the federal courts to investigate their own leaks. The upshot of this embarrassing media circus, in which the accused ranged from spies to magistrates, was, as journalist Raúl "Tuny" Kollman put it, that "*the Court said 'I did not do it' (but 'investigate me'), the Wiretapping Committee said 'I did not do it' and so did all the judges*" in charge of the so-called criminal investigations.

As an open ending, it is important to clarify that wiretaps are currently still in the hands of the Court and DAJUDECO, although there are increasingly strong voices demanding their return to the Prosecutor's Office. For now, the fate of communications interceptions in Argentina seems reluctant to clear itself a path.

12   The (Ab)use of Pretrial Detention

But this is still not the full extent of *shameful Law of criminal procedure*. Let us remember that being treated as innocent until proven guilty is one of the structural premises of any state that respects the fundamental rights of individuals (the constitutional Rule of Law). This means that, in order to apply a penalty, the state must first try the accused (respecting the guarantee of prior trial contained in Article 18 of the National Constitution of Argentina, and in the vast majority of all constitutional documents throughout the world)[55] and prove that he or she is guilty. In addition, the criminal conviction must be challengeable by means of, at minimum, an ordinary and effective appeal that allows for the broadest possible review. Thus, until there is no final sentence, no state penalty can be applied.

At present, the most serious penalty provided for in the Argentine Criminal Code is imprisonment, as set forth in Article 5. According to this article, deprivation of liberty during the course of the proceedings must be applied only in extremely exceptional situations, since otherwise it would function as an anticipated penalty. The rule, therefore, is freedom during the trial. Certainly there are provisions that allow for the restrictions of personal liberty as a means to achieve certain procedural, instrumental and precautionary purposes. For example, Article 280 of the Code of Criminal Procedure of the Nation permits the restriction of personal freedom when it is essential to ensure the discovery of the truth and the proper application of the law. However, Article 17 of the Code of Federal Criminal Procedure establishes that decisions to preemptively restrict an individual's liberty must be based on the existence of a real danger of flight or of hindering the investigation.

In short, the deprivation of liberty as a precautionary measure is appropriate only in rare exceptions. The aforementioned Article 17 of the Federal Code of Criminal Procedures clarifies that, for it to be applied, there must be sufficient evidence to charge the person with a crime punishable by deprivation of liberty; this is meant to prevent the use of coercive measure without substantial evidence, and to ensure that the measure is proportional with the potential penalty that might result from the trial (pretrial detention cannot be imposed, for example, if the person is charged with a crime that only provides for a fine or a penalty restricting rights or both).

The need for proportionality serves as a limit, but in itself it is inadequate to justify the deprivation of liberty during a trial. As stated in the "Díaz Bessone"

---

55   http://servicios.infoleg.gob.ar/infolegInternet/anexos/0-4999/804/norma.htm.

Plenary of what was then known as the National Chamber of Criminal Cassation,[56] release or exemption from imprisonment – that is, freedom – cannot be denied solely on the basis of the prosecution's claims (specifically, in that instance, the impossibility of a conditional sentence or a sentence of more than eight years).

13   On Delegitimization and Pretrial Detention

Of course, logically, when a penalty is imposed, the time already spent in detention is discounted as a precautionary measure, and, also logically, the mere act of putting an individual on trial is already a penalty in itself. Nevertheless it should be clear that pretrial detention should never be used as a preemptive punishment because it contradicts the principle of the presumption of innocence.

Consequently, the procedural risk, as a legitimate justification for pretrial detention, must be based on the personal circumstances surrounding the specific case, and demonstrate the defendant's intention to evade or impede the investigation. Moreover, to order a pre-trial detention, it is also necessary to consider whether or not, in the specific case, one might adopt some other, less burdensome precautionary measure. (For example, any of the guarantees provided for in the procedural order, such as the prohibition to leave a certain territorial area, the retention of documents, the obligation to appear periodically, submission to the care or supervision of a person, electronic surveillance, house arrest, and so forth.)

In short, pre-trial detention is designed to ensure that the person accused in a criminal case does not obstruct the investigation, is present during the trial, and will, at the time of sentencing, be available to appear before the judge. More than ever before, our procedural system includes a wide range of measures aimed at respecting the general principle of freedom during the trial. And if certain restrictions are considered essential, they range from the least to the most onerous, restricting ambulatory liberty only when it is clearly demonstrable that a less drastic alternative would be inadequate.

To summarize, the principles that govern pretrial detention and that, in turn, act as limits to it are: a) material merit, b) proportionality, c) exceptionality, d) provisionality, e) judicial control and review, and f) temporariness.[57]

---

56   http://www.saij.gob.ar/camara-nacional-casacion-penal-federal-ciudad-autonoma-bue nos-aires-diaz-bessone-ramon-genaro-recurso-inaplicabilidad-ley-fa08261043-2008-10 -30/123456789-340-1628-oots-eupmocsollaf.

57   Julio B. J. Maier. *Derecho procesal penal*. Editores del Puerto, Buenos Aires,1996.

This means that, for a person to be subject to pretrial detention, there must be a concrete probability of having committed the punishable act; that, if convicted, a prison sentence is expected; that confinement is the only way to neutralize the risk of flight or of hindering the investigation; that the measure is reviewed periodically; that it is carried out in dignified conditions and understood that, after a certain period of time, its reasons will no longer exist. Respecting these principles throughout the trial and until a final sentence is handed down is the only way to fully guarantee the principle of the presumption of innocence.

So much for the theory.

14   Violating the Rules of Pretrial Detention

In practice, pretrial detention is used in most cases for separate and distinct ends (anticipation of punishment), as a means of neutralizing the alleged "offender" (to prevent him from committing future crimes), for political purposes (to please those in power and persecute their rivals, social leaders, and dissidents, etc.), and even for social purposes (to give the community a false sense of security and police efficacy). It is interesting to note how preventive imprisonment appropriates the discourses traditionally attributed to the justifications of punishment, such as general prevention, special prevention, retribution, etc. In other words, imprisonment and pretrial detention are not only equivalent in real life, but also in idealistic discourses.

Anyone can be a victim of a criminal act, and this seems to entitle us to express an opinion on how to deal with crime. This is curious, because anyone can also get sick, yet this does give us all the right to make medical diagnoses. However, in criminal matters, the social mood has set the tone for most of the reforms produced and, at present, it is quite satisfied with *shameful Law of criminal procedure*'s imprisonment of people it deems necessary to neutralize for opposing the ruling power, be they petty thieves or corrupt "bigtime national crooks." (It should be added that these typologies are far removed from the exemplary white man that one sees on the covers of magazines, married with children, a businessman who only happens to have entered into politics.)

Although prisoners are very diverse, the way they are included in the *shameful Law of criminal procedure* tends to be similar. For example, if a singularly violent criminal event occurs and is heavily covered by the media, society reacts by repudiating it; in fact, attention is focused only on certain criminal acts because of their repetition, modality, etc. Complaints reach the political class, and so begins a "crusade against insecurity," the ideal platform for obtaining votes.

For their part, the people who complain invariably do so with the same purpose: they seek justice, which, in popular terms, is satisfied with harsher penalties and restricting the rights of the accused to their minimum expression. The result of all this is achieved when legislators pass laws that increase the number of crimes, increase the applicable penalties, or incorporate presumptions that allow deprivation of liberty prior to conviction without admitting proof to the contrary. However, since it is never possible to completely abandon the theoretical foundations of the constitutional Rule of Law – the only way would be to replace it with a totalitarian state – the constitutional and conventional principles, rights and guarantees live on, in a constant tension with ideas that, consciously or unconsciously, are those of a police state.[58]

15   Prison Punishments

In this context, pretrial detention is offered as a quick "solution" to every problem. Theoretical limits are blurred because the practice imposes its own limits. This forced confinement is manipulated in order to give society the impression that the offender has been caught and is now paying for his crime, to neutralize a threat and, in recent times, to "fight the corruption" of whoever just lost the election. As soon as the cameras stop filming, it hardly matters if the person detained – in some cases for years – proves in the end to be innocent.

Although it must be justified in each specific case, in recent years we have witnessed the imposition of preventive detentions guided by the same criterion, which in Argentine journalism is now known as the "*Irurzun Doctrine*,"[59] and refers to the practice of detaining the accused for having belonged to a political group that no longer governs, but who may still retain certain "functional links" that might hinder the investigation of a case. As we have already discussed, this practice is utterly inconsistent with the constitutional interpretation of this measure, since no one has been able to explain how this connection would generate a procedural risk. The origin of this way of "justifying" the precautionary detention of former government officials dates back to 2017.

During the same political period, we find another political weapon of *shameful Law of criminal procedure*: the direct application of physical – and of

---

58   Zaffaroni, Alagia y Slokar, *op cit.*

59   https://www.academia.edu/39724505/Prisi%C3%B3n_preventiva_y_doctrina_Irurzun.

course psychological – suffering through the use of imprisonment. Some brief conclusions would certainly be fitting here, but surely by now it is clear how there is a *shameful* criminal law and Law of criminal procedure for some; and a *true criminal law and Law of criminal procedure* (with constitutional guarantees) for others. Almost a friend-enemy dialectic. Hasn't it always been like this? Yes, we know. Won't it always be like this? Well, we hope to possess the means of correcting the sad course which criminal law and criminal procedure seem predestined to take. The question this historical moment presents us is, will we be able to do it?

CHAPTER 3

The Destruction of Criminology

Valeria Vegh Weis

1   The Criminal Case as a Strategy of Governance

At this point it is clear that the theory of crime and Law of criminal procedure cannot be analyzed, considered or criticized outside of the political, social and economic contexts in which they are inscribed.[1] In particular, their political use (and even the essentially political dimension of "technical" discourses, sources and programs)[2] cannot be separated from the world that surrounds them, under penalty of depriving them of their historicity.[3] This is why this chapter will employ a critical methodology in order to delve into the world of criminology, which will allow us to debunk the myth of neutrality that characterizes idealistic penal and procedural discourses,[4] and to consider the difficulties of lawfare from a broader social perspective, one coherent with reality. Key questions include: why is punitivity used to remove political adversaries? Why have those who wish to rid Latin America of populism and who view the market as the only guide to the port of free competition and entrepreneurship decided to dismember *true criminal* and *Law of criminal procedure*?[5]

There are times when the traditional politics of inclusive democratic debate, the transparent discussion of state policies, and even elections themselves do

---

1 Cf. Baratta, Alessandro. Criminología y dogmática penal. Pasado y futuro del modelo integral de la ciencia penal. En: *Revista de Sociología*, 13. 1980. pp. 13–48.

2 As evidenced by Zaffaroni, Eugenio Raúl. *Derecho penal humano y poder en el siglo XXI*. Trad. Rodrigo Murad do Prado. 1ª ed. São Paulo: Tirant lo Blanch, 2021. pp. 17 y ss.

3 We have already had occasion to understand where this *pretension of dogmatic sterility of law* leads, where it comes from and what it is for, and even its eminently political dimension. For further discussion on how it is not possible to dissociate the penal system from the socioeconomic system see Vegh Weis, *Marxism and Criminology. A History of Criminal Selectivity*, Brill, 2017. See also Andrade, Vera Regina Pereira de. Derecho penal: entre el mito de la neutralidad y la politicidad, el camaleón del poder punitivo. In: Boldt, Raphael [org] Teoría crítica y derecho penal. 1st ed. Belo Horizonte: São Paulo: D'Placido, 2020.

4 See the development in Baratta, Alessandro. *Criminology* (op. cit.).

5 See also Valim, Rafael. *Estado de excepción*: la forma jurídica del neoliberalismo. 1ª ed. Editora Contracorrente, 2017.

not seem to serve the objectives of the local representatives of imperialism[6] and transnational finance capital. Faced with this situation, Latin America has seen on countless occasions how those who wield political and economic power resort to the traditional military coup, but this alternative has clearly fallen into disuse (though it was never discarded, as witnessed recently in Bolivia[7] or in the political assassination of the Rio de Janeiro councilor Marielle Franco).[8] As already mentioned in the introduction, the subsidiary to traditional political violence is so-called *lawfare*.[9] This implies that long before resorting to the traditional coup or to political assassinations, the preferred option is what we might call *selective inoculation*, that is, targeting those who challenge the neoliberal agenda by accusing them of corruption, treason, illegal administration, or some other grandiose misrepresentation, and then putting them out of play by using the criminal justice system as a political weapon.[10]

Corruption, of course, is a systemic problem in Latin America (and probably on the planet), but the practitioners of lawfare are not exactly idealists dreaming of a better world. They seek to use punitive measures to get rid of those who think differently and occupy the seats of power or, if they are already in power, to continue governing under their agenda. As we have seen in recent years in Latin America, financial power uses lawfare not only to gain control of the executive branch, but also to stay in power and to rid their path of any opponent who might obstruct its neoliberal economic policies. In short, the criminal issue and the use of uncontrolled punitivity today are key governance strategies for those who, out of self-interest or as representatives of transnational financial capital, wish to impose the neoliberal model at any cost. What is a strategy? The simple and concatenated execution of different actions designed to achieve a certain tactical end.

---

6   In the wake of what Lenin had already called the "higher stage of capitalism." See the development of the idea in Lenin, Vladimir Ilich. *Imperialism, superior stage of capitalism.* Trad. Édições Avante! and Paula Vaz de Almeida. 1st ed. São Paulo: Boitempo, 2021.

7   Cf. Zaffaroni, Eugenio Raúl. Entrevista a Eugenio Raúl Zaffaroni Bolivia: Golpe de Estado al presidente indio. por Conrado Yasenza, La Tecla Eñe. 19 de noviembre. Aveilable at: <https://lateclaenerevista.com/entrevista-a-eugenio-raul-zaffaroni-bolivia-golpe-de -estado-al-presidente-indio-por-conrado-yasenza/>.date of access 12/12/2021.

8   Miranda, David. ¿Quién ordenó el asesinato de Marielle Franco? Mar./2019. Aveilable at: <https://www.theguardian.com/commentisfree/2019/mar/14/marielle-franco-murder -brazil>.date of access 12/12/2021.

9   Vegh Weis, Valeria. *El lawfare. (op. cit.).*

10   Rusconi, Maximiliano. *Crisis del derecho penal en la región*: selectividad social vs. selectividad ideológica. 19 de julio. Aveilable in: <https://www.infobae.com/america/opinion /2019/07/15/crisis-del-derecho-penal-en-la-region-selectividad-social-vs-selectividad-ide ologica/>...date of access 12/12/2021; VEGH WEIS, Valeria. *El lawfare. (op. cit.).*

It is important to note that the opponent need not be a total revolutionary. Small objections to the agenda of finance capital are enough to unleash judicial war. It could be the defense of natural resources such as oil in Venezuela, or the legalization of the coca leaf in Bolivia, the refusal to allow international organizations to intervene in the local economies of Argentina, the proposal of timid measures to redistribute wealth in Paraguay, or simply speaking of the Patria Grande or of independence from the United States in Ecuador. Before these acts of defiance, the courts become the place to settle power disputes that cannot be won at the ballot box, in congress, or in the houses of government. This is evident when political leaders from a certain side of the political spectrum at the top of elections are effectively embroiled in high-profile media accusations at key political moments. Examples include Cristina Fernández de Kirchner being charged in ten criminal cases in Argentina at key election moments; the parliamentary impeachment of Dilma Rousseff in Brazil and the preventive detention of Lula just before national elections; the criminal prosecution of Rafael Correa as soon as he left the office of the presidency in Ecuador; the allegations against the son of former Chilean President Michelle Bachelet for influence peddling; the criminal cases against Evo Morales and his officials in Bolivia; the impeachment and accusations of nepotism and overpricing made against Fernando Lugo in Paraguay; the Supreme Court's endorsement of the impeachment of the head of state Manuel Zelaya in Honduras; the Odebrecht case attacks that ended in the resignation of the president of Peru, Pedro Pablo Kuczynski; and the incessant attacks and accusations of corruption against the president of Venezuela, Nicolás Maduro, among others.[11]

The "fight against corruption" is the common denominator, "[t]he construction of a discourse, of a narrative, cohesive and unified in each of the proceedings and in all the countries."[12] But did corruption emerge and spread throughout Latin America at the same time, and just when social democratic or progressive governments were in power, ending their mandates, or leading the electoral polls? And did a militant commitment against corruption suddenly spread spontaneously in response throughout Latin America? In his book *Political Judgments of the President and the New Political Instability,*

---

11   Estepa, Constanza y Maisonnave, Marcelo (2020) "Poder Judicial, medios de comuni-
       cación y política: Lawfare en Argentina," *Nullius,* v. 1, n. 2, pp. 70–89.
12   Rusconi, Maximiliano (2019) Crisis del derecho penal en la región: selectividad social
       vs selectividad ideológica, *Infobae,* Jul. 15, https://www.infobae.com/america/opinion
       /2019/07/15/crisis-del-derecho-penalen-la-region-selectividad-social-vs-selectividad-ide
       ologica/.

Aníbal Pérez-Liñán[13] presents data from the Foreign Broadcast Information Service, which collects media reports from all Latin American countries. The data show that, in the early 1980s, there were only eleven reports of corruption in Latin America, but that just ten years later, the number suddenly reached two hundred. So did corruption increase? Apparently not. This increase "does not prove that corruption has become more widespread; it shows, rather, that accusations in the media have become more frequent," says Pérez-Liñán.

What really seems to be happening is that accusations of corruption are proliferating with a new social function: to operate as the sword while the courts act as the new battlefield, as already predicted by the texts responsible for the insertion of the concept of lawfare in the global north. In other words, it is no longer a matter of shooting or poisoning the political adversary, but of using the judicial system to judicially delegitimize those who resist the rule of the empire. If possible, it is even a matter of putting them in prison to remove them physically and electorally from circulation without running the risk that the population will change its mind and support them again, ruining the whole plan. In sum, punitivity has been reconfigured and, when the democratic electoral dispute is not enough, it operates by seeking the legal and political death of the popular opponent. To produce this political death, the objective is to erode the power of the adversary, to delegitimize him, to turn him into the cause of all the country's ills in the eyes of public opinion and the population. To produce this legal death, in the name of democracy those in power make effective use of preventive sentences and other penalties that will disqualify their opponents from ever again participating in politics.

2 Governing through Crime

The regional scope of the phenomenon, and the accusations of discretionary corruption not as an end in themselves, but as pretext within the framework of a global geopolitical agenda, contribute to our understanding of lawfare as a "governance strategy." This concept was proposed by the American critical criminologist and University of Berkeley professor Jonathan Simon.[14] He was referring to a situation very different from the one we are analyzing here, but it is useful to reflect on it.

---

13   Peréz-Liñan, Aníbal. *Juicio político al presidente y nueva inestabilidad política en América Latina,* Fondo de Cultura Económica, 2009.

14   Simon, Jonathan (2007) *Governing Through Crime: How the War on Crime Transformed American Democracy and Created a Culture of Fear.* NY: OUP.

Simon explains that, since the 1970s, there has been a change in U.S. (and world) politics: the distribution of wealth, access to education and healthcare and other social justice issues were removed from the public agenda in the name of a "national emergency" consisting of an increase in common crimes (robberies, homicides, assaults). It was not a question of any real emergency or increase in common crime, but rather of instilling fear and a "feeling of insecurity"[15] to create panic, bewilderment, and confusion, to make citizens believe that there were indeed thieves and murderers everywhere and that, consequently, there was no choice but to give carte blanche to those in power to deal with the issue, while problems related to education, health and equity were put on the backburner.[16]

He adds that the "war on crime" had the effect of concentrating power in the Public Prosecutor's Office: "the war on crime reshaped the American prosecutor into an important model for political authority while also giving real prosecutors enormous jurisdiction over the welfare of communities with little attention to the lack of democratic accountability."[17] Since then, prosecutors have come to be seen as the representatives of civic interest and of the victims, and as the great moral opponents of the defendants, jeopardizing the constitutional guarantees that protect the latter.

The victims of these crimes were another key factor. Those responsible for punitivizing politics portrayed them as bitter and merciless beings whose thirst for revenge would only be quenched with the application of the harshest penalties. Such was the use governments made of these victims that they even lent their name to new laws that increased the penalty for certain crimes, or imposed harsher conditions of imprisonment. The phenomenon described by Simon has also occurred in Latin America. For example, in Brazil, following the murder of Judge Patricia Accioli in Rio de Janeiro, the National Congress enacted Law 12.694/2021 named after the victim. More recently, Law 14.245/2021, baptized as "Mariana Ferrer Law," amended the country's Criminal Code and Criminal Procedure Code after the young Mariana was attacked during the trial. Law 11.343/06, "Maria da Penha Law," is also a product of this "insertion" of the victim into the discourses of criminal law.

Including the name of the victim runs the risk of using private loss to reaffirm the state's punitivity, and seems inadequate as an instrument of protection. If

---

15   Kessler, Gabriel (2009) *El sentimiento de inseguridad. Sociología del temor al delito.* Buenos Aires: Siglo XXI.

16   Batista, Vera Malaguti. *O medo na cidade do Rio de Janeiro*: dois tempos de uma história. Río de Janeiro: Revan, 2003.

17   Simon, Jonathan. *Governing through Crime*, p. 33.

Anton Bauer, a few centuries ago (going back to the first chapter), did not have at his disposal the means of investigation necessary for evaluating the effectiveness of punishment, today we have them. And critical criminology, from both the political-ideological and the scientific and pragmatic points of view, shows that the protective efficacy of punishment is minimal. Legislation based on the pain of the victim only ends up appropriating the conflict and even the victim himself in the name of an ideal justice that, in practice, does not diminish the prevailing victimization.[18]

Now, regarding Simon's thesis, recent times have witnessed a change in the type of crime instrumentalized to generate fear in citizens and to rule over any other issue without people protesting or remembering what is really important. It used to be the fear of the African-American teenager in the United States, or the child thief in our local version. The fear of crime has now yielded to the cultivation of anger at the corrupt or sellout politician. "There is *an emergency!*" "*Politicians are corrupt and the corrupt are the cause of all evils!*" they shout, and while the horrified public is busy complaining, state money flees to tax havens, education is destroyed, and the country is indebted for generations to come.

In other words, within the neoliberal lawfare paradigm, the specific crime invoked to stupefy the population with false emergencies is corruption. Here again, the resolution of the problem is placed in the hands of star judges and prosecutors in the federal jurisdiction, while the victims are the citizenry as a whole. The governance strategy is redirected specifically to the crime of corruption as a mechanism to morally isolate the accused, to reaffirm the judiciary as the legitimate representative of the citizens "ripped off" by these supposedly corrupt leaders, and to create a media spectacle capable of holding the public's attention while measures that impose a neoliberal agenda to the detriment of social justice go unnoticed.

Just as Jonathan Simon warned us about the use of common crime as a government strategy in the last century, today we are warning about the use of accusations of white-collar crime by opposition politicians as a governance strategy in the 21st century. In both cases the strategy is the same: to use the discourse of crime to distract the citizenry so as to govern without inconvenience. If we add this to a *post-democratic*[19] situation in which economic power

---

18   On punitive change in the last century, see also Garland, David. *La cultura del control, la delincuencia y el orden social en la sociedad contemporánea.* Nueva York, 2011; Wacquant, Loïc. *Les Prisons de la misère.* París, 1999; Wacquant, Loïc. *Castigar a los pobres: el gobierno neoliberal de la inseguridad social.* Durham, 2009.

19   Cf. Casara, Rubens. *Estado posdemocrático: neo-obscurantismo y gestión de los indeseables.* Civilização Brasileira, 2017.

is sometimes superior to the power of sovereign states,[20] the greater the risk that a criminal policy driven by imperial interests will determine the fears and priorities of a terrified citizenry.

3   Critical Criminology and the Political-Media Use of the Criminal
         Justice System

We have said that criminology can help us understand this complex situation, and that Jonathan Simon is a criminologist, but what exactly is criminology and what does it have to do with governance? For that matter, what does criminology have to do with the use of the criminal justice system as a strategy of governance? Criminology is, broadly speaking, knowledge that helps us understand how crime, the offender, punishment, and the socioeconomic system in which all this is framed work together.[21]

Up until the 1960s, the different criminological schools that then existed focused mainly on crime and criminals. These schools included the Enlightenment, Positivism (which we will discuss in more detail), and some early attempts at sociology. If someone posed the problem of corruption to the criminologists of the time, they would surely have studied only the allegedly corrupt (perhaps they would have even measured his skull) and the behaviors he was accused of, without thinking about the penal system, the biases of judges,[22] or the role of the mass media. Crime and delinquency. At most, the so-called Chicago School and the School of Criminal Subcultures, which emerged during the first half of the 20th century, would have considered the social circle and the places of work and residence of the accused, but not much more.

Then, in the 1960s, a breakthrough finally occurred when so-called Labeling Theory emerged. The most famous member of this school is Howard Becker,[23] who continues to write excellent books on research

---

20   Davis, K.; Fisher, A.; Kingsbury, B,; Merry, S. Gobernanza por indicadores. Oxford: Oxford
      University Press, 2015; Zaffaroni, Eugenio Raúl. *El Nuevo ...* (*op. cit.*). pp. 95 y ss.

21   For those less accustomed to criminological thought in general, an introductory hand-
      book with the full historical, descriptive and general prescriptive overview is Santos,Juárez
      Cirino dos. *Criminología: contribución a la crítica de la economía del castigo.* Tirant lo
      Blanch, 2021. For an introduction to the development of criminology in Latin America,
      see Del Olmo, Rosa. *América Latina y su criminología.* Río de Janeiro: Revan: ICC, 2004.

22   Cf. Vegh Weis, Valeria; White, Rob. *Una perspectiva marxista sobre la Agenda 2030 para
      el Desarrollo Sostenible.* En: Blaustein, Jarret [et. al.] [eds.]. Emerald *Handbook of Crime,
      Justice and Sustainable Development.* Esmeralda, pp. 63–68.

23   Becker, Howard. *Outsiders: estudios de sociología de la desviación.* Nueva York: 1963.

methodology.[24] Becker warns that there are many behaviors that do not affect anyone besides the person who performs them, and yet are considered crimes. This sociologist went to jazz clubs and interacted with marijuana smokers, and found that they were not disturbing anyone. People were just there, hanging out, thinking about life, music, existence. ... Becker asked himself: why do these behaviors constitute a crime? There he warns that what decides whether an action is criminal or not has less to do with its intrinsic conditions than with the *label* attached to it by the criminal justice system. For example, in many U.S. states, marijuana use is legal. How can it be that smoking marijuana in one state is a crime and across the border it is not? The State of Colorado says "*smoking marijuana is not a crime,*" while Louisiana says "*yes, it is a crime.*" That is, by crossing an avenue or road, the same conduct goes from being a legal action to a crime, demonstrating that there is nothing intrinsically evil about it. Rather, its legality depends on discretionary criminal policy decisions. In another example from not so many years ago, the Argentine criminal justice system stated that if the rapist married the woman he had raped, then the *label* of crime was removed from the action and it would be forgotten. Rape was still rape, but everything changed because the penal system decided to take off one label and put on another: "rape" became "marriage." These examples show that whether or not something is a crime has less to do with its supposedly evil nature and more to do with the label it is given. In other words, while since the dawn of modernity, the law has been presented as objective, rational and neutral, it is in reality a catalog of political-legal decisions that reflect the values of a given place and time.

What labeling theory needed was to go a step further and ask (and demand) *why* certain labels apply and others do not. The criminological school that would eventually explore this issue and put an end, once and for all, to the myopic vision of crime and the penal system, was called Critical Criminology. Emerging in the 1970s,[25] it was the first theory of criminology that aspired to a global scope. While the previous schools had developed mainly in the United States, Italy, Spain, France or Germany, Critical Criminology developed simultaneously in Europe, the United States and Latin America. In all three places, there formed associations of Critical Criminologists who realized that, if one really wanted to understand crime and punishment, one had to analyze the

---

24   Cf. v.g., Becker, Howard. *El trabajo sociológico: método y sustancia.* Londres: Routledge, 1970; Becker, Howard. *Trucos del oficio: cómo pensar en su investigación mientras la realiza.* Chicago: University of Chicago Press, 2008.

25   Cf. Walton, Paul; Young, Jock. *La nueva criminología: por una teoría social de la desviación.* 2ª ed.

capitalist production system, the struggles for power, colonialism, and the unequal distribution of resources between the North and the South of the planet. This school is the one that today allows us to see that the State of Colorado is earning many tax dollars with the legalization of marijuana consumption and that it was the correlation of forces between Democrats and Republicans that made possible the fight for legalization. In short, it is thanks to Critical Criminology that, when we see an accusation of corruption today, we can move the magnifying glass away from the accused and take into account all the many other interests involved.

4   How to Build a Good Case

Eduard Bernays was the nephew of Sigmund Freud (whom we will discuss later). He was also a publicist and journalist. He was born in Vienna, but settled in the United States. There he was a member of the Creel Commission, a government propaganda delegation set up to influence public opinion and gain public support for the entry of the United States into World War I. Based on this experience, as well as on his uncle Sigmund's work on the unconscious, Bernays plunged into the honeyed waters of persuasion and mass manipulation. The result was his 1928 book *Propaganda*. He writes: *"The conscious and intelligent manipulation of the organized opinions and habits is an important element in a democratic society. Those who manipulate this unseen mechanism of society constitute an invisible government which is the true ruling power of our country. We are governed, our minds molded, our tastes formed, our ideas suggested, largely by men we have never heard of."*[26] He understood quite clearly that if propaganda could be used for war, it was also possible to use it for peace.

Throughout the 20th century, many have taken these lessons to heart. There are countless examples of press campaigns, uses of propaganda, spreading rumors, spying and selling information to achieve political objectives. We only have to remember the campaigns of the two world wars, the Cold War, the Vietnam or the Gulf War, or the press operations in the Malvinas War, which told us that we were winning while young Argentines were dying of cold and hunger at the end of the world. These propaganda mechanisms became even more complex with the televising of armed confrontations, which contributed both to their spectacularization and to the demonization of the enemy. With this came the use of news of dubious origin, known today as *fake news*. The

---

26   Bernays, Edward L. *Propaganda*. 1928. p. 9.

format and technology have changed, but the pattern of permanence is and has always been the same: those men we have never heard of and whose faces we will never see determine our lives from the shadows, as Eduard Bernays, the father of public relations, once predicted.[27]

Let us consider how all of this applies to today's governance in Latin America. We have already discussed the disastrous effects of Nazism on *true criminal law*. Let us explore this a little further. Joseph Goebbels, the well-known Propaganda Minister of the Nazi regime, did not care so much about the law itself as he did about the message. He explained that in order to have an effective message that captivates the public, you have to choose a single enemy and convey hatred through a single idea or symbol. He called this principle the *"principle of simplification and the single enemy."* In today's terms, a concrete enemy: "the Kirchners (the Ks)," "the Workers' Party (PT)," "Chavismo," "Populism," and so on. Once the adversary has been chosen, as Goebbels would say, it is necessary to hit the same nail many times. In the current scenario in Latin America, this is: *"corrupt, corrupt, corrupt!"* Then, following Goebbels's teachings, comes the "principle *of the contagion method:*" all adversaries must be made to fall into the same category (an individualized collective). This is an observable reality, as the mass media places "Latin American corruption," "Latin American populism," and "Latin American regimes," including those of Cuba and Chile, all within the same category. There is also the *"orchestration principle,"* or the importance of tireless repetition of simple messages, always highlighting the same concept and without fissures. Hence the famous phrase: *"if a lie is repeated often enough, it ends up becoming the truth."* Thus we often find ourselves saying phrases that are not our own only as a result of the media bombardment that constantly reiterates them until they become a mantra. In Argentina, for example, people find themselves today, thanks to the *"orchestration principle,"* repeating *"they stole two GDP "* to refer to the government of Néstor and Cristina Fernández de Kirchner (2003–2015) even though they have no idea that the acronym stands for "gross domestic product" or what that means.

---

27   Fake news reached a particularly risky dimension in the context of the COVID-19 pandemic. All over the world there were many examples of people with supposedly high credibility spreading information contrary to scientific innovations. Even the current President of Brazil, Jair Bolsonaro, propagated remedies of proven ineffectiveness for the treatment of the disease. (see EL OBSERVADOR. Viviana Canosa was fined for "attacking public health" in her program. August/2021. Available at: <https://www.elobservador.com .uy/nota/viviana-canosa-fue-multada-por-atentar-contra-la-salud-publica-en-su-progr ama-202189163410>. Accessed 12/12/2021).

Goebbels also warned of the *"transfusion principle,"* i.e. that lies cannot be constructed out of nothing. Propaganda must always be linked to something pre-existing, be it traditional hatreds or prejudices, preconceived ideas or national mythologies. It is a question of shutting down meaning, spreading arguments who derive their power from the primitive attitudes of yesteryear. Ideas like *"progressives have always stolen everything,"* or *"those who defend them are all lazy bums living off welfare checks"* work very well with pre-existing class hatreds. Last but not least, according to Goebbels, is the *"singularity principle,"* which is nothing more than convincing many people that what they think coincides with what everyone else thinks and must, therefore, be true. It is the famous and well-known *"everybody knows they are corrupt."* Proof? No need, because "everybody knows it."

In short, a bit of history to understand how to build a case and create a certain impression in the characterization of Latin American politicians in order to put them on trial while the public applauds without asking why.

5   The Law of the Criminal Act and the Law of the Criminal Perpetrator

To circumvent the constitutional guarantees protecting citizens from the abuse of power, Goebbels and the Nazis relied on the "healthy sentiment of the good German people," a wild card to violate any pre-existing right. In 21st-century democracies, this same discursive logic is often used in the daily media in a more subtle way.

The first issue is the *criminal perpetrator* versus the *criminal act*. Modern criminal law is a law of the *criminal act*, which means that the law punishes people insofar as they commit a prohibited human conduct, and not because of their thoughts or personality.[28] In short: *without action there is no crime.*[29] One can dream all one wants of killing one's boss, but if one does not grab the knife and stick it in (or, at least, show it while threatening to kill him), criminal law does not apply.

---

28   Batista, Nilo. *Introducción crítica al derecho penal brasileño.* 12ª ed. rev. e atual. Río de Janeiro: Revan, 2011. pp. 89 y ss.

29   For a development on the historical trajectory and importance of the theory of action, see Rocha, Renato Gomes de Araújo. *Teorías de la conducta: antecedentes, tendencias e impases.* – 1. ed – Río de Janeiro: Revan, 2016; Radbruch, Gustav. *El concepto de acción y su importancia para el sistema del Derecho penal.* Trad. José Luis Guzmán Dalbora. Buenos Aires: Editorial B de F, 2011.

Nazi criminal law, by contrast, was a *law of the criminal perpetrator,*[30] punishing people not for what they did, but for who they were. As we said in the first two chapters, they were condemned for being Jews, for belonging to the LGBTQIA + community, for being Jehovah's Witnesses, Communists, Socialists, Sinti and Roma, Slavs, Soviets or disabled persons, i.e., regardless of what they had (or had not) done. The question was one of *being,* not of *doing* or *not doing.* The German criminal lawyer Edmund Mezger wrote of this: *"in the future there will be two (or more) 'criminal rights:' a criminal law for the majority (in which the principles that have prevailed up to now will continue to apply) and a (completely different) criminal law for special groups of certain persons, such as, for example, delinquent types [...]. Once 'special criminal law' (that is, indefinite imprisonment) is included, it must be applied without limitations and, from that moment on, all legal differentiations become pointless."*[31]

This *law of the criminal perpetrator* is today considered incompatible with the social and democratic rule of law, in view of the fact that the state has no authority to interfere in the most private spheres of people's subjectivity. In general, we call this political-legal postulate *the harm principle* or *the offense principle.* It can be stated as the right of every citizen to be as morally reprehensible as he may be, and this moral autonomy remains protected from the legal interferences of the State up until the concrete moment in which these immoralities (and of course this definition is, in itself, very controversial) are translated into an objective and external behavior, that is, into a *conduct,* a *human action.* In Argentina, according to Article 19 of the National Constitution, *"the private actions of men that in no way offend public order and morals, nor harm a third party, are answerable only to God and exempt from the authority of the magistrates. No inhabitant of the Nation shall be obliged to do what the law does not command, nor deprived of what it does not prohibit."* The theoretical development of the category of the dignity of the human person in

---

30   Zaffaroni, Eugenio Raúl. *La doctrina* ... (*op. cit.*).

31   This theoretical conception is, in short, the one that was later recovered, in some form, by the followers of what has been called "criminal law of the enemy." On Mezger, see Muñoz Conde, Francisco, *Edmund* (op. cit.). Cf. also Grispigni, Filippo; Mezger, Edmund. *La reforma* ... (*op. cit.*) as well as Mezger, Edmund. *Criminal Law.* In Brazil, it was Aníbal Bruno who introduced Mezgerian thought into the national doctrine. Bruno knew Mezger's work and was the main disseminator of the "psychological-normative" conception of guilt among Brazilian penalists. See, on this point, Batista, Nilo. One hundred years of reprobation. In: Batista, Nilo; Nascimiento, André [orgs.] *Cien años de reprobación: una contribución transdisciplinaria a la crisis de la culpabilidad.* Rio de Janeiro: Revan, 2011. pp. 167–168.

Brazilian constitutional literature also leaves no room for doubt.[32] In Latin it can be summarized as: *nullum crimen, nulla poena sine lege.*

In addition to the fact that no one can be punished for merely being or existing, thinking or believing, no one can be punished for what he does if that action does not affect a third person (to this denomination is also due the *harm principle,* but also all the theoretical development of the *theory of the legal good*),[33] and no one can be punished if, prior to the act, the crime was not clearly described in the criminal law so that the person would know what to do or not to do before acting (here we have the most basic political-legal postulate of *true criminal law,* the so-called *principle of legality*).[34] From this it also follows that it does not matter how ill-tempered or perverse the person in question is: if he has not committed an action prohibited by law, there is no way to open the floodgates of punitivity. We can say, then, that all these tenets form a visible and powerful barrier between morality and the law that should govern the daily activity of the courts in criminal matters.[35]

As we pointed out at the beginning of the book, the usual criminal offenses in lawfare cases (and which can open the floodgates of punitivity) are illicit enrichment, prevarication, incompatible negotiations, malicious omission, legal exactions, embezzlement, bribery, tax or financial crimes, misappropriation of public funds, receiving an undue advantage, transnational bribery,

---

32   Cf. Sarmiento, Daniel. *Dignidad de la persona humana: contenido, trayectorias y metodología.* Belo Horizonte: Editora Fórum, 2016.

33   See for example Tavares, Juárez. *Teoria do injusto penal.* 4ª ed. São Paulo: Tirant lo Blanch, 2019; Tavares, Juárez. *Fundamentos de teoría del delito.* 3ª ed. São Paulo: Tirant lo Blanch, 2020; Santos, Humberto Souza. *¿Sigue viva la teoría del bien jurídico?Una contribución al debate sobre la teoría del bien jurídico y los límites materiales del poder estatal de incriminación.* São Paulo: Marcial Pons, 2020.

34   Its systematic formulation, as we know it today, is an important chapter in the work of Anselm Feuerbach. Cf. Feuerbach, Paul Johann Anselm Ritter von.*Tratado de derecho penal* 1st ed. Buenos Aires: Hammurabi, 2007. Trans. Eugenio Raúl Zaffaroni and Irma Hagemeier; Feuerbach, Paul Johann Anselm Ritter von. *Anti-Hobbes: o sobre los límites del poder supremo y el derecho de coacción del ciudadano contra el soberano.* Trad. Leonardo Brond. 1st ed. Buenos Aires: Hammurabi, 2010. Even today, this German contractualist criminalist continues to arouse the interest of jurists, who have not ceased to study him. Cf. for example, Greco, Luis. *Lo vivo y lo muerto en la teoría de la pena de Feuerbach: una contribución al debate actual sobre los fundamentos del Derecho penal.* Madrid: Marcial Pons, 2015; Queiroz, Rafael. Mafei Rabeb. *La teoría penal de P. J. A. Feuerbach y los juristas brasileños del siglo XIX: la construcción del derecho penal contemporáneo en la obra de P. J. A. Feuerbach y su consolidación entre los penalistas de Brasil.* 2009. Thesis (Doctorate in Philosophy and General Theory of Law) – Law School, University of São Paulo, São Paulo, 2009.

35   Cf. Batista, Nilo. *Cien. (op. cit.).*

influence peddling, and fraud against public administration, among others. When the evidence is very weak, the accusation may end up as the "breach of duties of a public official," a crime that includes any deviation from his obligations as an official and that puts in check the limits of the *true criminal law*.

When the use of punitivity appears as a strategy of governance, constitutional guarantees disappear and the criminal *law of the perpetrator* is imposed, not on the basis of what the person does, but on the basis of what the person is. The emphasis is placed on personality: whether you wear brand name clothes, the tone of your voice, whether you are bossy or arrogant; what you do or do not do remains in the background, and with it, *the law of the act* is forgotten along with the constitutional guarantees.

Moreover, the unimportance of the criminal charge itself can also be observed here. It is unlikely that the citizenry understands or remembers the type of crime of which those who are on the docket today are accused. Everything is subsumed to a judgment about the person: we repeat, he is corrupt. In this way, the most important guarantee of *true criminal law* in the rule of law goes unnoticed, that is, a clear accusation based on prior criminal law, as established in Article 18 of the National Constitution of Argentina and in similar regulations in the rest of the world. It is possible to downplay the crime to concentrate on the "guilty" person since the opposing media and politicians (and even the courts) omit any legal technique and mix the whole thing into a big "salad" to such an extent that the fact itself is not understood, much less the criminal charge or the characteristics of the judicial process. Another technique often used by the single party media monopolies is to ignore official sources, to resort to rumors and hearsay and, above all, to decontextualize verified information. In short, all this could be theorized in the real sense of "muddying the field." It is about putting the spotlight and glare on "who" is the protagonist of the news (who is the offender?, *the law of the criminal perpetrator*) over the fact itself (i.e. the "what" of the event, *the law of the act* that must prevail if we respect constitutional law).

Such is the lack of centrality of the actual charge that a common strategy is what could be called *drop-by-drop prosecution*. If there is no relevant criminal fact to be charged, multiple accusations are levied for many different acts, even when it is known that most of them will not succeed, even with the help of the collaborating judge. The idea is that the public is constantly bombarded with information about new cases, which creates in the "public opinion" the idea that the charges are endless and the situation is terrible and unmanageable and very serious. Any ordinary person would think, when turning on the TV, *"Well, this person must really be the worst politician, otherwise he would not be talked about so much!"*

All this without mentioning the effects that all this produces at the unconscious level. That is to say, the repetition of facts in the media delegitimizes the politician in question in the public imagination. Moreover, thanks to the media monopolies (let us recall once again the studies already cited by Perseu Abramo), it is enough to negotiate with one of them for the news to multiply infinitely. With the internet and social networks, this viralization is even faster, more diffuse, and more powerful. It does not matter what is denounced, as long as there is a photo of the entrance of the courts, a person explaining that he is presenting the accusation, and many media constantly reproducing it. Drop by drop, the glass gets fuller. For example, in Argentina, on February 25, 2019, the former President of the Nation, Cristina Fernández de Kirchner was summoned to testify in eight different cases on the same day. The media monopoly (and opponents of the former president) described the day as an "atypical day" and a "marathon morning of interrogations." The facts charged were not the center of the news, only the number of cases and the phrase "multiple accusations" permanently pelted the ears of a citizenry that was never presented with the facts of cases that, later, were archived due to lack of evidence.

6   The Role of the Judge

Who is the executioner of this program of the political and legal death of the adversary? There is a state power very well suited to the task. It deals with individuals and acts with surgical precision and without any need of armies, blows or blood: the judiciary. Just as Labeling Theory showed that very few behaviors are intrinsically harmful, a consideration of the tactics of lawfare shows that, in a similar sense, judges are not impartial gods or the rational applicators of the law, but rather the spokespersons of jurisdictional decisions that endorse or discredit certain interpretations of the law. In this sense, when the supreme court confirms a sentence or declares someone guilty, it is not an absolute truth. There are political interests and ideological positions behind every jurisprudential pronouncement. Moreover, these considerations are not limited to "political cases" with officials or leaders involved. Every decision made by a judge is political, even in trivial cases such as theft. One judge may decide that the person shoplifted out of necessity and therefore does not deserve punishment due to mitigating circumstances,[36] while another may say that

---

36   Zaffaroni, Raúl (2007) Culpabilidad por la vulnerabilidad, SAIJ, http://www.saij.gob.ar /doctrina/dacfo70010-zaffaroni-culpabilidadporvulnerabilidad.htm.

private property was affected, that nothing justifies this action, and declare the defendant guilty as charged.[37]

Returning to lawfare, many judges collaborate with this mechanism of governance in the hopes of gaining positions, promotions, or an increased staff or budget. If that does not work, many end up collaborating when threatened with the obstruction of promotions or complaints of poor performance. When lawfare cases fail to be adjudicated to these judges using the jurisdictional rules imposed by law (e.g., lotteries), there are numerous examples of the manipulation of the rules of competition. In Argentina, even the famous mathematician Adrián Paenza spoke about it. The journalist Horacio Verbitsky asked the mathematician what were the chances that nine of the ten cases against former President Cristina Fernández de Kirchner would have been "drawn by lot," as they were, and fallen to only one of the twelve federal courts. Paenza explained that, mathematically, if there were ten cases and twelve judgeships, the chances that nine of the ten drawn cases would fall to only one were 0.000000001777%.[38] As one can see, the judiciary is incredible. It even defies the laws of mathematics.

Moreover, the judiciary has sufficient authority to accumulate several categories of crime and mold them into the construction of multiple criminal cases, even when they are based on flimsy evidence that will eventually be overturned in the higher courts. The judiciary can also file cases or leave them idle according to the needs of the political moment. Thus, even though the constitutional guarantee of equality before the law requires that all persons be treated equally, this does not occur in ordinary cases and even less so in lawfare cases. For example, in Argentine federal court cases (where complaints against public officials are investigated), cases take more than three years to be resolved and less than ten percent reach trial. However, when it comes to lawfare cases where there is a determined political intentionality, the cases are quickly resolved as soon as the time is right.

Returning to the *law of the criminal act*, judges have to demonstrate the facts of the case before imposing a sentence (in adversarial systems, the collection of such evidence is up to the prosecutors). It must be clearly shown that the act

---

37   Vegh Weis, Valeria y White, Rob (2020) A Marxist Perspective on the 2030 Agenda for Sustainable Development, en Blaustein, Jarret et al. (eds.) *Emerald Handbook of Crime, Justice and Sustainable Development,* Emerald, pp. 63–83.

38   *PERFIL. El cálculo matemático que hicieron Paenza y Verbitsky sobre Cristina Kirchner y Claudio Bonadio.* Abril de 2019. Aveilable at: <https://www.perfil.com/noticias/politica /calculo-matematico-que-hizo-adrian-paenza-horacio-verbitsky-sobre-cristina-kirch ner-y-claudio-bonadio.phtml>. .date of access 12/12/2021.

occurred and that the defendant committed it with knowledge of what he was doing, and without any justification. All of this is governed by the general theory of the crime. This theory states that the accusation must have as its object a conduct (voluntary human action), and this conduct must be prohibited by law (either the Penal Code or the special criminal laws describing the crime and the corresponding sanction), anti-juridical (it must not be permitted by law, as in the case of self-defense and state of necessity), and culpable (i.e. for the conduct to be imputed to the accused, he must have known the unlawfulness of the action and must not have been subjected to any serious coercion that would prevent the free manifestation of his will).[39]

There are many filters to overcome, but, in lawfare cases, it is not necessary that the judicial activity culminate in an effective conviction where all guarantees have been respected. To achieve the delegitimization of the political opponent, it is enough that his name and the criminalizing judicial language ("arrested," "charged," "multiple accusations," "guilty") are associated and exhaustively repeated, even if it is never proven that a crime has been committed. Once the accusation has been presented and the case has been reproduced in the media and remains open, it is not essential to reach a judicial conviction. The media conviction will have already taken place.

There may not even be a need for any judicial activity at all, just an abstract statement to the effect that at some point the criminal justice system will be involved. An example of this can be seen in the cover story of the most widely circulated newspaper in Argentina. The headline stated that Alberto Fernández [the current President of the nation and at that time presidential candidate] "would be accused" as an organizer of an conspiracy.[40] This headline was published only three days after the announcement of his candidacy, significantly delegitimizing his figure. The accusation was that he had worked out a strategy with a member of the Supreme Court to prevent the trial of the former president and his current running mate, Cristina Fernández de Kirchner. However, nothing was known about the nature of this purely mediatic accusation. The only relevant thing was the political *timing*: producing content to condition the mood of an audience immediately after the pre-election announcement and associating the name of the political enemy with a criminal case.

Moreover, as long as the political and legal death of officials influences concrete political and electoral disputes delimited in time, they do not require a

---

39   Zaffaroni, Raúl, Alagia, Alejandro y Slokar, Alejandro (2002) *op cit.*
40   Clarín, Denunciarán a Alberto Fernández como "organizador" de una asociación ilícita por el caso D'Alessio, 21/5/2019, https://www.clarin.com/politica/denunciaran-alberto -fernandez-organizador-asociacion-ilicita-caso-alessiooUYG8zgZj2.html.

firm conviction. What is relevant is to remove key leaders from the political game at decisive moments (a moment of social upheaval, an election). In this sense, a subsequent nullity or revocation of a conviction does not affect the good health of lawfare. This is complemented by the fact that lawfare not only affects the person specifically identified as a target, but also operates as a Sword of Damocles to discipline all those who might follow a similar ideological line.

7   Corruption and Other Moral Panics

Even with the activity of the judiciary, the citizenry could reject these rumors or even think they do not matter if the socio-economic situation was better under the person labeled as "corrupt." That is, the citizen could say *"what do I care if there is corruption when I am better off than before, when I can buy myself a car and pay the bills?"* However, the media also invokes patriotic sentiment, honesty, honor, and any other value that can be molded according to the desired objectives of presenting a new cosmic evil. This generates a fear of such magnitude that it could be called "panic," and influences thoughts, feelings and opinions in a way that could be called "moral."

In the 1970s, Stanley Cohen, criminologist and professor at the London School of Economics, coined the phrase "moral panic." The professor explained that certain episodes, people or groups become amplified, distorted, exaggerated to the point of representing terrible threats to the values of society, prompting a collective reaction process. These alarms are not innocuous. They are functional to the interests of powerful groups. He explains how in the mass media their nature is presented in a stereotypical way; editors, bishops, politicians and other right-thinking people are in charge of erecting moral barriers; experts are consulted and issue their diagnosis and solution. Sometimes, Cohen continues, the panic passes and falls into oblivion, while at other times, it has more serious and lasting repercussions and may even produce changes in legal and social policies or even in the way society conceives itself.[41]

Like Jonathan Simon, Cohen was thinking about street crime, about common crimes (robberies, thefts, drug dealing in the neighborhood). We have experienced this many times in the global south and north. In Argentina, a great moral panic was aroused by a specific bank robbery in which a pregnant woman was shot, resulting in a miscarriage. Although such situations are rare,

---

41   Cohen, Stanley (2001) *States of Denial: Knowing about Atrocities and Suffering,* Oxford: Blackwell.

the repercussions of this case were such that the regulations in force in banks were modified, and today it is still illegal to use a cell phone on bank premises, as this was the means of communication used by the accused.[42]

The subject that brings us together in this book allows us to expand Cohen's concept of "moral panic" to include accusations against public officials in lawfare cases. The mechanism is the same: what good citizen does not feel morally outraged upon learning of the misuse of his or her taxes? The accusations and the magnitude of the danger are overstated (*"they are all corrupt,"* *"Iranian terrorists will run free and unpunished all over the world,"* *"they have stolen everything"*) until they create a level of alarm that horrifies and paralyzes the population, opening the floodgates of punitivity. According to Cohen, the power groups determine which deviation becomes an emergency (for example, "corruption"), distorting it to the point that it becomes a modern demon that devours everything ("the cancer of corruption"). This dynamic then requires exaggeration ("the scandal of corruption"), speculation ("everyone is corrupt and it is inevitable") and negative symbolization (stereotyped politicians and photos with taglines like "the lost image").[43]

In the third edition of his book, Stanley Cohen regretted a bit the term "panic," thinking that perhaps it was too drastic. But when applied to the Latin American reality, the word may prove to be correct. Ideas like "corruption" or "treason" are a sword in the hearts of citizens manipulated by so much misinformation. So they fall into a scandalized panic and cry out in desperation, as we have already pointed out: *"they have stolen two GDP s."*

The unequivocal question is: who is providing the disinformation that creates all this panic? This "moral panic" mechanism, Cohen explains, requires "moral entrepreneurs" who define the conflict as a tragedy, an emergency against the collective interests of both sides, and demand an urgent response. "Moral entrepreneurs" set the agenda by selecting accusations against public officials as the most important issue of the day, by devoting most of the news to covering them, and by transmitting images that reinforce the idea of "emergency."[44]

---

42   Infobae, A 10 años del asalto a Carolina Píparo, el caso bisagra que cambió la seguridad en los bancos: "Sigue siendo mi obsesión el porqué de tanta violencia," 29/07/2020, https://www.infobae.com/sociedad/policiales/2020/07/29/a-10-anos-del-asalto-a-carolina-piparo-el-caso-bisagra-que-cambio-la-seguridad-en-los-bancos-sigue-siendo-mi-obsesion-el-por-que-de-tanta-violencia/.

43   Cohen *op. cit.*

44   Cohen *op. cit.*

In our modern societies, the biggest "moral entrepreneurs" are the media (discussed below). The media are so important that they are often recognized as "the fourth branch" (along with the Executive, Legislative and Judicial). They wield a significant and growing influence on the behavior of individuals and social groups, modifying attitudes and thoughts by manipulating the discourse.[45] What is more, they spread these panics while presenting themselves as neutral representatives of public opinion, reaffirming the credibility of the news. The "moral panics" encouraged by the "moral entrepreneurs" condense the political struggles to control the means of cultural reproduction.[46] These words explain how any citizen can end up effectively hating a particular political figure and swearing passionately that he or she was corrupt without being able to present any proof of these accusations.

Following Cohen, our argument is that accusations of corruption become "moral panics" with which to pressure and condition a government to carry out (or not) a certain policy or render it impossible. If the enemy is in the opposition, it is also an effective means of destroying him politically, so that he cannot even compete for a lesser prize. Moral panics are important when neoliberal governments are in power because, by labeling the opposition as corrupt, they serve to delegitimize those who are critical of the neoliberal economic agenda. In either case, moral panics unleash a social reaction in the citizenry that is disproportionate, exaggerated, irrational, and unjustified with respect to the seriousness of the problem and the aim of achieving extra-legal effects functional to neoliberal governance.

It is worth quoting Jaime Durán Barba, ideological advisor to the neoliberal government led by Mauricio Macri, who governed Argentina between 2015 and 2019. In his book *The Art of Winning*, Durán Barba said: *"we should not get lost in legal technicalities because, for ordinary people, every politician is guilty even if proven otherwise* [...] *Regardless of whether judges declare the accused innocent or guilty, if communication is poorly managed, there is always the feeling that 'something sketchy was happening.'"* For these reasons, the political consultant recommends that, in the face of attacks, it is not worth giving legal answers, that is, answers based on current legal codes. Instead, the solution is to have a very good legal defense, but also to keep in mind that *"nowadays values have deteriorated and public opinion even influences judicial sentences. Politics is*

---

45   Julianne Schultz, *Reviving the Fourth Estate: Democracy, Accountability and the Media*, Cambridge University Press, 1998.

46   Antonio Gramsci, *Prison Notebooks*, Columbia University Press, 2011.

politics. That is why the leader must make his case for the people and the media, while his lawyers make theirs before the magistrates."[47]

Constitutional guarantees (or "legal technicalities," in Durán Barba's language) are less important. What is more important is the social alarm, the spread of "moral panic" and the pointing of fingers (at others, not at oneself).

8   Preparing the Audience

In order for the anti-corruption message to reach citizens and for them to "identify" with that idea or image, an audience must be created. And the audience is made up of people. And people are all different. But they are also all the same.

This, which at first sight seems a paradox, is exactly that: the *"paradox of identification."* This concept was elaborated by Sigmund Freud, a Viennese thinker and physician who created the field of psychoanalysis around 1900. Freud explained that what we call "personality" or "identity" is what differentiates us from others, but is constituted based on our "identification" with others. In other words, we are all different in our desires, choices, and experiences, but we are all the same in our need to identify with others.

The mechanism of "identification" allows the constitution of what we call "the self" of each of us. The "I" constitutes the personality or identity, the voice we hear when we speak. From the perspective of the French psychoanalyst Jacques Lacan, we could even say that there is no possible identity for the subject, that we are different subjects every time we speak because our identity depends neither more nor less than on the articulation between signifiers. "Identity" is then nothing like an "essence," nor does it carry any inherent attributes. It is only a mirage that allows us to enunciate "I am such and such," a response to a "structural lack."[48] In this conception, the subject is a lack, much like the game Sudoku. The most important thing in this game is the empty space between the numbers because that is what allows the others to be inserted in order to win the game. Well, for Lacan this is the subject: the empty space, the lack, which moves with each movement and which is the product of a game of signifiers. Upon this lack, this hole, an "identity" is constructed out

---

47   Todo en Durán Barba, Jaime; Nieto, Santiago. *El arte de ganar: cómo usar el ataque en campañas electorales exitosas.* 1ª ed. Buenos Aires: Debate, 2011.

48   Lacan, Jacques. *La identificación. Seminario 1961–1962.* Recife: Centro de Estudios Freudianos de Recife, 2003.

of the successive "identifications," and it is with this identity that we relate to others.[49]

In Freud's thinking, meanwhile, the "ego" is constructed through the superposition of "identifications," which Freud himself compares to the layers of an onion. He tells us that the "ego" has conscious parts (what we know about ourselves) and unconscious parts (to which we will never have access by reasoning). These are the "id" and the "superego" which, together with the "ego," complete the psychic apparatus.

The "id" is the instinct that commands us to eat a dozen desserts even if we have diabetes, and the "superego" is the judge that we all have inside us who punishes us for eating the desserts and even for desiring them. The "ego" is the referee who attempts to manage all this pressure.

Following Freudian-Lacanian principles and returning to the example of the onion, the idea is that if all our "identifications" (the layers of the onion) fall off, we discover that underneath them there is nothing, there is an empty space (Lacan would say that there is something: there is a "lack," that of the subject). But this only happens after many years of analysis and, besides, it is always possible to add layers. How are these new layers formed? From certain experiences that happen in and to each body, the traces left by what we have "seen and heard."[50]

It is in the traces left by the "seen and heard" that the agents of lawfare do their work. How? By offering to a public subject to the daily vicissitudes of life under capitalism (work, home, responsibilities) specific models of identification (in general, beautiful blond millionaires). This "identification" plays a role in the constitution of our "identities." Psychoanalysis does not tell us why one person identifies with one model and another with its opposite, but it gives us a clue: within each person there operates an enigmatic *"unfathomable decision of the self."* Each person makes decisions regarding his subjective position at a moment he will never be able to remember (a mythical moment). It is a decision made in the unconscious (so we have no access to it). There are the prejudices, the tastes, the pleasures, those things that happen to us and that we cannot explain, that "chemistry" that we feel before a certain thing (or person), and the visceral hatred that we feel before another.

Let's say, then, that "identity" is, by definition, a mirage, a blank screen on which things that do not exist are reflected. It is not necessary that the figure with whom we identify share any characteristics with us, it is only necessary

49   Lacan, Jacques. *La identificación (op. cit).*
50   Freud, Sigmund. *La interpretación de los sueños.* Trad. Paulo César de Souza. En: Freud, Sigmund. Obras completas. Vol. 4. 1ª ed. São Paulo: Companhia das Letras, 2019.

that we believe or want to share traits with them (the so-called *"aspirational identification"*). Thus, nothing prevents an employee of a supermarket chain from identifying with a television diva who opposes the four-day workweek that would materially benefit the worker. The public turns on the TV, reads the newspaper, looks at the cell phone or buys a magazine and there he sees himself, by means of identification with certain characteristics (those indicated by his *unfathomable decision*), although the material reality shows another scenario.

We always need others to include us in the culture, because this is what allows us to "be a person." Our market culture offers us certain models constituted on the basis of certain shared (or imposed?) ideals, such as the diva in the previous example. The "identification" mechanism then acts as it will with those models. Consultants (to which some politicians turn when campaigning) and marketing firms are specifically tasked with building an effective model that meets the aspirations most valued by the sector they are targeting. With this enormous volume of information and images, we end up forming yet another layer in our onion. Thus the experience between people, and between people and things, can easily be exploited by an advertising agenda managed by the usual people. That is how an audience is formed. Or, to put it another way, the formation and consolidation of a social subject is established in such a way as to favor the interests of the few.

How would Freud explain why it is that people continue to believe the media, consulting firms, and advertising companies when they do not offer any proof of what they claim? Freud would say that it is a matter of "projection" and "idealization." "Projection" coincides with love. In fact, initially Freud believed that "projection love" could be reduced to what happens inside the psychoanalyst's office during the session, but later he was convinced that love is love in all cases. All "love" is "projection" and all "projection of knowledge" (attributing knowledge about something to another) is "love." "Idealization," in turn, consists in attributing to someone the qualities we need him to have so that we can idealize him.[51]

We return to a question that has already been raised. Is it possible that all this confusion of identification, projection, and idealization is so strong that a person might end up voting or acting against their own interests? Can it be that prominent members of the LGBTQIA + community have passionately supported Jair Bolsonaro in Brazil, despite the fact that he has declared a thousand and one times that homosexuality seems to him an abomination? The answer,

---

51   Freud, *op cit.*

unfortunately, is yes. Not infrequently, men and women support actions and people that will bring very negative consequences in their lives. Freud explains how people act against themselves in his famous text *Totem and Taboo*.[52]

Freud tells us there that one of the characteristics of the human species is to stumble twice (and a thousand) times over the same stone (to return to the place where we were made to suffer). Neurotic guilt and self-punishment – the work of the superego – are mechanisms that constitute our psyche. As we mentioned with the dessert example, it is not necessary to commit an inappropriate act for the full weight of our superego to fall on us. In other words, in order to condemn oneself, it is not necessary to have committed a transgression in real life; it is enough to have done so in a fantasy to be punished (the point is that the superego always knows our infractions, even the most imaginary ones, because it is part of us). It is enough to have desired candy, even if we end up eating an apple, for self-punishment to rule the day.

If we know that the superego will punish us even if we have only desired what is forbidden (desire is always contrary to the law), we have only to conveniently redirect the guilt that already exists. Let us remember that we already have the models in which an unsuspecting public has already deposited many of its "identification" ideals. Now the agents of the financial system and their local allies are taking advantage of the situation, offering a number of good reasons (good for them) to make people feel guilty. They also offer an array of sufferings to allow the public to atone for their guilt. For example, they declare it unacceptable for the poor to freely use electricity and pay affordable prices for it, or that the right to paid vacation be guaranteed to everyone. The idea is that even the poor person who can finally turn on the air conditioning on a 110-degree day feels so guilty that he cries to his superego, considering himself unworthy of the model to which he aspires. The catch is that, for the superego, one is never worthy, one is always guilty of something.

And since everyone already feels guilty for something, all that need be done is direct it appropriately. If Oedipus blinded himself out of guilt, what other people are willing to do will depend on how one manages to manipulate their fears, their desires, and their frustrations. This is how people can hate those who gave them a credit for the air conditioner, and even themselves for daring to turn it on. It is the structure of neurosis: we are all guilty before our "superego;" the situation, manipulated by the media, international interests, judges and consulting firms, simply provides the content of the punishment.

---

52   Freud, Sigmund (1918), *Totem and Taboo*, Cosimo Classics, 2009.

9   The Importance of Media Criminology

Notwithstanding the geopolitical and normative complexity of the processes described above, media conglomerates approach the issue without any regard for the basic tenets of criminology. Following a corporate agenda of which they often form only a small part, the communicators (and not the experts) are the ones who tell us who the offender is, what the crime is, and what punishment it deserves. In this way, voluntarily or involuntarily, the media reaffirm distorted ideas about crime and punishment as if they were absolute truths (*fake news*) in what is called "media criminology."[53] By this means, the facts and the outcome of the trial are transmitted in the words and concepts of communicators who become the sole translator and bridge between an isolated judiciary and a citizenry deprived of the service of justice.

Television, radio, newspapers and all major media work towards achieving the greatest possible exposure. And they achieve it by depicting shocking images of the enemy engaged in some sort of suspicious behavior. If there are no incriminating photos or videos, it is enough to show the enemy behaving suspiciously. We can even accuse our enemy of owning an asset that does not belong to him, as happened with former President Lula da Silva in Brazil.[54] TV anchors have gone so far as to construct actual masonry vaults in the studio, arguing that former Argentine president Cristina Fernandez de Kirchner would have hidden ones like these on her property.

In other words, focused as they are on creating and perpetuating moral panics, media criminology is characterized by its disregard for specific legal knowledge and by its tolerance of the dissemination of incorrect information. Every media spokesperson is free to express their opinion on how to reform justice or curb corruption, not for the purpose of providing validated information, but rather to generate the greatest media impact against certain leaders. The facts of the case, the nature of the accusation, and the responsibility of the accused are not usually the focus. Instead, the news is at the service of lawfare as a strategy of governance, and remains indifferent as to what really happens on a judicial level in the case.

---

53   Zaffaroni, Raúl (2011) *La Cuestión Criminal, op cit.*
54   Batista, Nilo. La defensa en tiempos oscuros. En: Zanin Martins, Cristiano; Zanin Martins, Valeska; Valim, Rafael [coords.] *El caso Lula: la lucha por la afirmación de los derechos fundamentales en Brasil.* São Paulo: Contracorrente, 2016. pp. 96–97; Yarochewsky, Leonardo Isaac. *Los medios de comunicación que atacan los proyectos garantistas.* Oct./2017. Aveilable in: <http://www.justificando.com/2017/10/31/midia-que-ataca-projetos-garantistas/>. Fecha de acceso: 21/11/2021.

For example, media spokespeople speak in general terms of "corruption," despite the fact that corruption as such is not a criminal offense. No precise information is conveyed as to whether the possible accusations refer to specific criminal offenses. Instead of providing the regulatory and judicial details of each case, or recognizing that corruption is a complex structural problem that besets all political parties and every society in the world, the problem is transformed into an emergency for the purposes of creating moral panic, reduced to slogans (e.g. "they stole two GDP"), and exclusively identified with certain political parties (e.g. "Kirchner corruption"). In this sense, the headlines chosen to disseminate lawfare news are fundamental. They are eye-catching and memorable, such as "Operation Car Wash" in Brazil or "The Notebook Scandal" in Argentina. The key idea is that the public, to whom the legal and factual details of the accusation are never explained, remembers the extravagant title of the scandal, the word "corruption," and the names of the persons denounced.

Nothing new under the sun. Since the dawn of modern history, but especially since the last dictatorship, we have learned that the media are far from neutral. During the last civil-military dictatorship in Argentina (1976–1983), the mainstream media used the term "confrontations" to describe the military's extrajudicial executions, thereby suggesting the idea of a fight between equals. The same media labeled the Grandmothers and Mothers of Plaza de Mayo (the associations of mothers and grandmothers searching for their detained or disappeared children and grandchildren) as "anti-Argentinean" for making personal demands while World Cup games were being played a few steps away from a torture and extermination center.[55]

In short, it is not enough to co-opt the judiciary and add more layers to the "identity onion" if the message does not spread into the streets. The media must amplify the information about the ongoing criminal case so as to turn it into a government strategy. Media criminology thus shows us the power of the media to define what crime is and how to combat it, without having any expert knowledge whatsoever.

The French-born sociologist Pierre Bourdieu, creator of structuralist constructivism, once explained this mechanism. He pointed out that television exercises a form of symbolic violence, with the tacit complicity of those who suffer it and even of those who practice it, insofar as both are not always aware of suffering or exercising it. Bourdieu has shown that television "conceals by showing," that is, by publishing something different from what it would have

---

55   The Relevance of Victims' Organizations in Transitional Justice Processes. The Case of
      Grandmothers of Plaza de Mayo in Argentina, Intercultural Human Rights Law Review,
      vol. 60, 2017, pp. 1–70.

to show if it were doing what it should do, namely, reporting what is really happening. Bourdieu also points out that television sometimes shows what it should show, but in such a way that it goes unnoticed or seems insignificant, or elaborates it in such a way that it acquires a meaning that does not correspond at all to reality. Television and the media in general do not focus so much on reality as on spectacle. They encourage the dramatization of events, they stage an event in images and exaggerate its importance and gravity, appealing to the public's sense of the dramatic, of the tragic (of the demonic, Stanley Cohen would say). The media, as moral entrepreneurs, become the representatives of a certain kind of morality, spiritual leaders who tell people what and how to think.

As the Italian political scientist Giovanni Sartori once said, such is the influence of the media on our way of thinking that instead of "homo *sapiens*" we have become "*homo videns.*" Television transforms reality (and our way of thinking), transfiguring information into images that arouse emotion and sensitivity instead of critical and reflective judgment. Television forges public opinion, which translates into feelings.[56] That is why many people know little or nothing about the actual accusations of corruption or treason, and yet feel such a visceral hatred for the accused that they cannot see the forest for the trees.

10   *Bots* and *Trolls: Influencer* Criminology

In the 21st century, television, radio and newspapers are not enough. "*Homo videns*" consumes, above all, the media transmitted by social networks. These networks provide a fundamental tool for the dissemination of the message. Not only do they work 24 hours a day, seven days a week, but they also have the advantage of anonymity: anyone can say whatever they want and they don't even have to be honest about their identity. When these networks create ideas about crime and punishment, we can refer to it as "influencer criminology."[57] Thus, much of the information we assimilate about what crime is, who the criminals are, and how to deal with this "scourge" is the result of scrolling on social networks. In Argentina, researchers Eugenia Mitchelstein, Pablo Boczkowski and Mora Matassi point out that social networks and websites are the second-most preferred option for news consumption among 18–29 year

---

56   Giovanni Sartori, *Homo Videns: La Sociedad Teledirigida,* Taurus, 2007.

57   Vegh Weis, Valeria (2021) *Criminología Influencer,* Página/12, Mar. 10, https://www.pagin a12.com.ar/328642-criminologia-influencer.

olds. In numbers, 69% of respondents with access to social networks (and 74% of those under 30) agreed with the phrase "I find news online while browsing social networks."[58]

It is enough to put keywords like "corruption + Latin America" in a search engine to realize that coverage is always an agenda item. The articles insist on signifiers such as "corruption," "bad government," "democratic erosion," "populism," and "institutional weakness." As we have seen, there is no rigorous analysis of the accusations or crimes themselves. In this way, the media acts to systematically violate the presumption of innocence, which indicates that it is not constitutional to impose punishment and use assertions about "guilty" or "convicted" until a judge has demonstrated, in a legitimate criminal process, that the person actually committed the act.

These posts and tweets can be created by anonymous individuals and even, going further, by employees hired specifically to post messages of a particular nature ("trolls"). A group of trolls can help to reaffirm the message that such-and-such an official has been convicted by using that keyword and confusing the other users of that social network, even when there has not yet been a conviction.[59] Additionally, there are the fake accounts: users who impersonate politicians, artists or other famous people. And the influencers: people with many followers who will read and even reproduce whatever the influencer posts. Sometimes, the messages are not even written by people, but by algorithms called bots. Bots serve, above all, to put certain topics on the agenda of the day or to generate noise by the number of messages they circulate. Of course, the bot language sometimes fails to translate properly. On one occasion, Mauricio Macri's party ended up publishing tweets that said *"meaningful caresses"* and *"satisfy Mauricio,"* and which ended up trending on Twitter (although not for the reasons sought) during the last presidential campaign in Argentina in 2015.[60] In this fashion, on any given day, when a sensitive issue is being voted on in parliament, *bots* can distract public opinion by turning an unfounded accusation of a politician into a *trending topic*.

---

58 Pablo J Boczkowski, Eugenia Mitchelstein, Mora Matassi, News comes across when I'm in a moment of leisure": Understanding the practices of incidental news consumption on social media, New Media & Society, 02/01/2018, https://journals.sagepub.com/doi/10.1177/1461444817750396.

59 Vegh Weis, Valeria. *Criminología influencer. Op cit.*

60 Infobae, "¡Satisface a Mauricio!," "caricia significativa" y otras frases insólitas viralizadas en Twitter abrieron un debate sobre los bots en campana, 9/8/2019, https://www.infobae.com/tecno/2019/08/09/satisface-a-mauricio-caricia-significativa-y-otras-frases-insolitas-viralizadas-en-twitter-abrieron-un-debate-sobre-los-bots-en-campana/.

This debate is not insignificant: an expert in digital trends, Mary Meeker, estimates that bots are responsible for almost half of the world's traffic on social networks.[61] In other words, half of the information consumed is created by algorithms designed to create meanings unrelated to the facts. Political scientist Natalia Zuazo explains this phenomenon in strictly economic terms: spreading false information against the adversary is cheap and fast; proactively doing high-quality journalism is expensive and takes time.[62]

How does this data relate to our topic? For example, a study on the national road case against the current vice-president of Argentina, Cristina Fernández de Kirchner, showed that 80% of the comments generated in the networks were created by *trolls*. That is to say that eight out of ten comments that spread through the networks and were consumed by unsuspecting users were produced by people hired to write them. *Influencer* criminology, by using both people and logarithms, acts as a complement to mass media criminology, expanding and disseminating information, presenting it as a joke, meme, *sticker*, *gif* or other form of entertainment. In this way, *influencer* criminology reaches more people and is consumed constantly and almost mechanically, giving the user the impression that it is merely entertainment when in fact the user is being fed a steady stream of data.

Media and influencer criminologies are fundamental to lawfare. A criminal case that is not effectively communicated and transmitted to the masses is pointless. Even a criminal case that will inevitably be closed due to lack of evidence can be useful to lawfare if, as long as it is active, it is broadcast to ordinary people and reaffirms the idea that the defendant is guilty. For this objective to be achieved, the success of the prosecution is not as important as the photo taken at the door of the courts when the complaint is filed, or the tweets and posts by the *trolls* and *bots* about a "new criminal case against x" without any explanation of the content. In the words of Rafael Bielsa and Pedro Peretti, "for infamy to materialize as a political fact, it must reach a mass audience ... Without a mass reach, discredit is reduced to village gossip, relatively harmless, and stripped of its potential to demolish, to explode onto the public sphere and hold captive the political scene."[63]

What with the moral panics and emergencies, the lack of validated information, the disregard for normative and jurisprudential knowledge of the case,

---

61   Mary Meeker, Internet Trends Report, 2019, https://www.bondcap.com/#archive.
62   Zuazo, Natalia. *Guerras de Internet: un viaje al centro de la red para entender cómo afecta a tu vida.* Buenos Aires: Debate, 2015; Revista Anfibia en http://revis¬taanfibia.com/ensayo/vivir-en-las-redes/.
63   Bielsa y Peretti, *op cit.*p. 10.

and the reduction of the news to discretionary slogans, a significant percentage of the citizenry now has no idea what is really going on. Citizens who work all day long and who also have families, friends and hobbies, probably do not have the time, the interest, or the preparation to see what goes on behind each news item, check if it is true and then mull the matter over for a long time. This is further complicated by the fact that even those interested in delving into the specific cases soon discover that the media networks have monopolized the information and that there are no other channels of communication between the people and the judiciary. In other words, ordinary people and the judiciary are completely separate worlds, united only by the bridge of media and influencer criminologies.

11   The Corrupt Must Look Corrupt

In addition to the judiciary, the "moral panics," the predisposition to self-punishment characteristic of the human psyche, and the media and social networks, there is also the issue of aesthetics. If one were to draw or imagine a criminal, what would he look like? Thinking about criminals in terms of unattractive images is part of the legacy of positivism.[64] This criminological school, established at the end of the 19th century by Cesar Lombroso, Enrico Ferri, and Rafael Garófalo, took upon itself the task of linking crime to aesthetic parameters of ugliness, brutality, and coarseness. The positivists would go visit prisons (full of poor people who, under the material conditions of confinement, lacked the resources to appear particularly beautiful) and then claim that these incarcerated people effectively represented the universe of criminals. They did not realize (or did not want to realize) that prisons only contain those whom the penal system has selected for punishment, and not every offender.[65] Positivism also shares with the Inquisition the image of the witch as the criminal par excellence. In short, both the Inquisition and positivism have contributed to the fact that today, when we hear or see the word "criminal," it is so difficult for us to envision stockbrokers who practice tax evasion.

The media are great at associating political enemies with ugliness. For example, the former President of Argentina Cristina Fernandez de Kircher was drawn in a monstrous caricature having an orgasm. Former Vice President Amado Boudou was photographed being arrested in the early hours of the

---

64   On criminological positivism, see Santos,Juárez Cirino dos. *A criminologia da repressão: crítica à criminologia positivista.* 2ª ed. São Paulo: Tirant lo Blanch, 2019.

65   Vegh Weis, Marxism and Criminology, *op cit.*

morning in his pajamas. Following the same formula, progressive politicians are consistently presented as informal, disheveled, without manners or respect for protocol; or, on the contrary, with exaggeratedly indulgent tastes that are supposedly incompatible with a progressive ideology. The counterpart is generally a model neoliberal businessman, usually blond and with a successful economic trajectory. Thus, the comparison between ugly and corrupt political enemies on the one hand, and the supposed efficiency of the model businessman rival becomes an effective tactic. *"If he can run a company, of course he can run a country!"*

The final blow: it is not enough that they are villains. The image must also catch them at their worst. The formerly powerful are now on the dock. The former minister is filmed while being arrested in his house slippers. The one who used to give orders now, surprisingly, begs for permission to receive medical treatment abroad so as not to die. It seems that history is cyclical. The masterpiece of yellow journalism was the coverage of the U.S.-Spanish war over Cuba in 1898. The campaign was conceived by William Randolph Hearst, owner of the newspaper the *New York Journal*, who was in stiff competition with Joseph Pulitzer and those who supported the liberation of Cuba. What did the Father of Yellow Journalism do to earn such a nickname? He distorted the news about the insurrection, encouraged the public to express their opinion, and sent his chief photographer to the island. After spending some time there, the chief photographer, Frederic Remington, started noticing that the reality was different from the one propagated by his newspaper, and sent a letter to his superior informing him of the situation and of his intention to return to New York. In response, Remington received a telegram that read: *"Please remain: you furnish the pictures and I'll furnish the war. W. R. Hearst."* Hearst furnished war to such an extent that he moved to Havana with some of his best reporters, artists, and photographers. At the end of the conflict, Spain was defeated and Cuba, Puerto Rico, the Philippines, and Guatemala became the dependent colonies of the United States, which also gained control of the strategic Panama Canal.

Hearst, who in the 19th century already understood so well the importance and attraction of an image, would have had a feast in the 21st century. Let us return to Durán Barba. In the aforementioned book *El Arte de Ganar* (*The Art of Winning*) he states that *"all of the research agrees that people vote based on the image of the candidates much more than they do so based on doctrines or proposals [...]. A photo of a candidate assaulting a woman [...] can cost him more votes than the neoliberal or socialist programs he defends."*[66]

---

66   Durán Barba, Jaime; Nieto, Santiago. *El ...* (*op. cit.*).

If ever a televised and photographed arrest would have made Hearst proud, it was, as we have already mentioned, that of former Vice President Amado Boudou. The procedure took place on the morning of Saturday, November 3, 2017. Hours later, the newspaper *La Nación* was already publishing the images. How did the opposition newspaper have access to so much visual material produced inside a private residence and only a few hours after the fact? However it may have happened, Boudou, who was described as a political enemy by *La Nación* and the defenders of the neoliberal agenda for having created the measure to nationalize the private pension system (the business of an elite few), appeared before the public in the living room of his house, in his underpants and socks, with bloodshot eyes.

As a result, many of the arrests of Latin American leaders have been excessively photographed and filmed as a result of extensive journalistic campaigns at the entrances to their homes. There have also been bursts of images of court appearances without the accompaniment of any accurate information. In short, the photograph of handcuffed hands – even if only for a second – is more interesting than the legal grounds or proven criminal liability. It is all about eroding *real criminal law* until it is "*shameful*" and fully subject to the invisible powers.

The great danger is that when the media and networks disseminate the image of a leader being arrested in pajamas in his living room, we are accepting that the right to privacy can be trampled without consequences. When the media and networks publish the content of phone calls between detained people and their lawyers, they legitimize the idea that there is no problem with turning private conversations between the accused and their lawyers into a public spectacle. When a "corruption scandal" is published without judicial proof that the person in question actually committed a crime, we are throwing out the window the principle of innocence until proven otherwise that protects every citizen. When it is announced in the media and networks without any criticism that once again another court case against such-and-such a leader fell by lot to the same judge, although it is mathematically impossible that all cases drawn by lot fall to the same court, we are ignoring the right to due process and the right to an impartial judge that is essential to any democracy. When we speak of "impunity" as soon as a complaint is filed without giving time for judicial investigation, the principles of innocence and due process are once again violated. Thus, lawfare not only operates against certain leaders, but also puts the whole democratic system at risk.

12   Criminal Selectivity

Many of the most troubling aspects of lawfare are manifest daily in the large number of criminal cases against common defendants (i.e., not officials or leaders) tried in our courts. The partiality of judges, the violation of due process, the anonymity of judicial officials, not knowing when the case will be resolved, the powerlessness before what should be a service of justice, and the abuse of pretrial detention are systematic problems of the criminal justice system. The difference with respect to lawfare cases is that these injustices go even more unnoticed because they affect the poor, the young, and people of color.

This observation reinforces the previous line about the use of the penal system as a strategy of governing both those "from below" (in ordinary cases) and those "from above," i.e., those who choose to represent the interests of marginalized sectors (in lawfare cases). In other words, the penal system persecutes the poorest groups and those who tend to defend their interests. Moreover, the over-criminalization of the marginalized (in ordinary cases) and of the leaders who to a greater or lesser extent defend their interests (in lawfare cases) is complemented by the under-criminalization of the powerful (in ordinary cases) and of the leaders who belong to this social group or who at least represent them in the political sphere (in lawfare cases). The selectivity of the penal system thus continues to be the fundamental ethical problem.

Indeed, the penal system has never been fair. Since the beginning of the capitalist production model, when the first courts appeared and the workhouses became the prototype of today's prisons, the clientele has always been the same: the poor and ethnic minorities.[67] The end effect is that criminalization has never responded to who produces more damage to humanity and to life on planet Earth, but rather functions to protect the process of capital accumulation and the concentration of wealth. What would a world be like in which polluting rivers was penalized by police agencies with more vehemence than selling drugs on public streets to compensate for the lack of employment? But that, for the moment, is only a dream. Today we live, as we did five centuries ago, under a penal system that neutralizes the surplus of the labor market, with the exception of some very scandalous cases that punitivity cannot ignore, mainly homicides. But even in these cases, the punitivity always looks first at the poor.

Empirically, it is enough to resort to the statistics elaborated by the Ministry of Justice. The characteristics of the prison population in Argentina, which are

---

67   Vegh Weis, Valeria, *Marxism and Criminology*, op cit.

no exception, show that most of those deprived of liberty are young people under 35 years of age, convicted of theft or attempted theft, who come from populous cities, with little or no education, who had a precarious employment situation or were unemployed at the time of incarceration and who, in general, had no professional training. The positivist criminologist Cesar Lombroso would see this and say that it is possible to conclude that all criminals are poor and uneducated. By now we know that this is a mistake, and that if the prisons are full of poor people it is because the punitivity knows very well how to turn a blind eye on the crimes of the powerful.

So it is worth asking why now, when the punitivity turns its attention to the corrupt, we write a book against it. It is true that in lawfare cases, criminalization is directed at certain people who do not belong to the group normally targeted by the punitivity. The point is that these cases are not an unprecedented awakening of justice in search of a more equitable system that prosecutes those who cause the most harm to the vast majority of humanity. It is not a sudden change that has resulted in the decision to put justice at the disposal of a better world by combating corruption.

It seems, in fact, that corruption in particular has not actually increased, and that the criminal cases related to this issue are far from constituting an epic of justice. On the contrary, it looks more like a governance strategy intended to ensure that those in power are those who defend the interests of the 1%, those committed to the neoliberal government program, those who do not want to leave even the crumbs to those who have the least, those who think that integrating into the world means becoming the pampered child of Washington DC and abandoning all dreams of regional emancipation. Meanwhile, the ones on the dock are those who, in different countries throughout the region, have tried, with greater or lesser vehemence, to prioritize the interests of their nations over those of the empire, to proclaim sovereignty and promote societies that are minimally fairer or more egalitarian, and all to the detriment of the invisible but palpable economic interests of large corporations and financial capital.

Another central aspect of lawfare that often goes unnoticed is that it is embedded in the general selectivity of the penal system. The selective mechanism is that which operates in ordinary jurisdiction through, on the one hand, laws, police, judiciary and penitentiary systems that prioritize the criminalization of poor young people, regardless of whether the crimes perpetrated are coarse acts against property or linked to consumption or micro-trafficking of drugs with little or no social harm (over-criminalization). On the other hand, selectivity implies that these same laws, police, judiciary, and penitentiary system minimize or exclude the criminalization of powerful people or those with higher social status, even if the crimes perpetrated are harmful acts with great social impact such as indebting the nation by embezzling its funds, or privatizing public spaces through incompatible negotiations, or environmental crimes (under-criminalization).[68]

Lawfare does not escape these dynamics of over- and under-criminalization. Through over-criminalization, lawfare seeks the political and legal death of progressive leaders. The prosecution of Lula da Silva is perhaps the exemplary instance of "lawfare by over-criminalization." Criminal law was abused by imposing on him a sentence that legally disqualified him from participating in politics and even deprived him of his physical freedom. Law of criminal procedure was abused through forum shopping, illegitimately used pretrial detention, illegal wiretapping, arbitrary evaluation of evidence, and violation of communications. Media criminology was abused through the use of the media and social networks to accuse him of a crime without evidence, discrediting his public image and his political career. In short, through "lawfare by over-criminalization," criminal law, Law of criminal procedure, and criminology were applied in a disproportionate manner with respect to the social damages falsely attributed to the former president in order to *threaten* his political and legal life.

In contrast, "lawfare by under-criminalization," which tends to go unnoticed in political-legal analyses, seeks to *save* from political and legal death the political leaders functional to the real economic power. Continuing with the case of Brazil, this concept shows that lawfare did not end with the nullity of the cases that originally caused the over-criminalization of Lula, but continues in the under-criminalization of Judge Sergio Moro and President Jair Bolsonaro himself, both involved in setting up the case against Lula. The situation in Argentina is similar in that, even when cases against former President Cristina Fernández de Kirchner such as the so-called "Future Dollars" case are dismissed[69] and key information about the judicial articulators (known as "judicial roundtable") comes to light, the "lawfare by under-criminalization" allows those responsible for the over-criminalization to remain unscathed by the punitivity.[70] The cases against leaders aligned with the neoliberal agenda

---

68   Vegh Weis, Valeria, *Marxism and Criminology, op cit.*

69   Vegh Weis, Valeria (2021d) *El sobreseimiento de Cristina y Axel: ¿Le ganamos al lawfare?,* Página/12, Abr. 13, https://www.pagina12.com.ar/335492-el-sobreseimiento-de-cristina-y -axel-le-ganamos-al-lawfare.

70   Ámbito (2021b) Persecución a Indalo: el método de Ercolini y Hornos para complacer intereses ajenos, Sep. 7, https://www.ambito.com/politica/grupo-indalo/persecucion-ind alo-el-metodo-ercolini-y-hornos-complacer-intereses-ajenos-n5270765.

are part of this logic, without prejudice to the great social damages they may have incurred, as shown in the cases involving Argentinean postal system or foreign debt levied against former President Mauricio Macri.[71] The media inexplicably protect the image of these leaders, hiding from the public the harmful deeds committed, and allowing them to tell the story in the way that best suits their candidacies.[72]

13   Intersectionality

The concept of intersectionality is key to delving deeper into this double standard of criminal selectivity.[73] This critical model recognizes that power and marginalization are intersected by class, social status, gender and skin color, among other factors. In other words, not all marginalized people suffer from over-criminalization in the same way. On the contrary, penal systems operate differently (and more harshly) against non-white, indigenous, and poor people. Of course, in terms of gender, women's incarceration rates are lower than men's, but this is largely a function of patriarchal social control: women are controlled by a wide range of social institutions ranging from the family to school and the neighborhood to media and religion, placing the penal system in a subsidiary role.[74] But what happens to women who escape the image shaped by patriarchal social control? What happens when strong, empowered women leaders occupy the center of the political agenda? When women disregard the "prescriptive aspects of the gender stereotype to which they are assigned" and occupy decision-making positions traditionally reserved for men, "it is possible

71   Lijalad, Ari (2021) Correo: la causa cumple 20 años y los Macri aún no pagaron, Sep. 19, https://www.eldestapeweb.com/politica/correo-argentino/correo-la-causa-cumple-20 -anos-y-los-macri-aun-no-pagaron-20219190550.

72   Cf. Semer, Marcelo. *El escudo de prensa permite a Moro contar la historia de Lava-Jato como quiera.* Diciembre/2021. Aveilable at: <https://www.brasil247.com/midia/marcelo-semer -escudo-da-imprensa-permite-a-moro-contar-historia-da-lava-jato-como-quer>. date of accessl 12/12/2021.

73   Crenshaw, Kimberle (1989) "Demarginalizing the Intersection of Race and Sex: A Black Feminist Critique of Antidiscrimination Doctrine, Feminist Theory and Antiracist Politics," University of Chicago Legal Forum: Vol. 1989: Iss. 1, Article 8. Available in: http://chicagounbound.uchicago.edu/uclf/vol1989/iss1/8.

74   Federici, Silvia (2009) *Caliban and the Witch. Women, the Body and Primitive Accumulation.* New York: Autonomedia.

to arouse discriminatory and hostile behavior against them."[75] And this is particularly evident in lawfare via the over-criminalization of women leaders.

The first strategy in these cases is usually to discredit the alleged leadership and attribute it to the "man next door." This happened with Cristina Fernández de Kirchner when she won the presidential elections of December 10, 2007, succeeding her husband, Néstor Kirchner. As Azar and Tavares da Motta state, "her arrival to power was preceded by a strong media campaign that referred to the 'presidential marriage' and warned that the real 'strong man of the government' would continue to be the former president."[76] Similarly, Dilma Rousseff's presidency in Brazil was presented as a puppet administration with Lula as the real power.

Subsidiarily, when the "man next door" strategy proves insufficient, punitivity, through lawfare, abandons the gender disparity with which it traditionally operates to deal with wayward women. That is, in contrast to the gender discrepancy in criminalization rates for ordinary crimes, women leaders, including former Argentine President Cristina Fernández de Kirchner, former Brazilian President Dilma Rousseff, former Argentine Attorney General Alejandra Gils Carbo, and Argentine social leader Milagro Sala, are targeted by lawfare for over-criminalization to the same extent as their male counterparts. Moreover, the characteristics of lawfare by over-criminalization when it comes to women have particular characteristics: the private sphere (which women should never have left, according to patriarchal ideology) becomes part of the over-criminalizing strategy: "the focus of treatment is shifted from political issues to issues of the private order. When it comes to women, personal appearance, family, motherhood, feelings, and intimacy become the central concerns of journalistic discourse."[77]

This inclusion of the private sphere privileges attacks on motherhood, with examples of media and influencer criminology publishing personal data of Gils Carbo's daughter,[78] or questioning the motherliness of Fernández de Kirchner

---

75   D'Adamo, Orlando et al. (2008) "Mujeres Candidatas: Percepción Pública del Liderazgo Femenino," *Revista de Psicología Social*, v. 23, n. 1.

76   Azar, Indiana Rocío y Tavares da Motta, Luiza (2020) *op cit.*

77   Pérez, S. y Aymá, A. (2017) *"Medios, Multimodalidad, Género y Política: Cristina Fernández de Kirchner en Noticias,"* Revista Observatorio, v. 3, n. 6, pp. 517–556, p. 527.

78   Perfil (2017) Clarín publicó el teléfono de la hija de Gils Carbó y ahora recibe amenazas, Oct. 13, https://www.perfil.com/noticias/politica/gils-carbo-dara-de-baja-el-celular-de -su-hija-porque-clarin-lo-hizo-publico.phtml.

by publishing private information about her daughter's health.[79] Likewise, attacks on the mental health of these women are included, such as accusing Fernández de Kirchner of being psychotic and perverse.[80] Even her sexuality is made public, as evidenced by the cover of *Noticias* magazine with a caricature of Fernández de Kirchner having an orgasm.[81]

Psychoanalysis also allows us to delve into this aspect. Women are attacked for their way of "being women." The onslaught is aimed at mercilessly exposing their defects and shortcomings in relation to the "ideal woman." But, as Freud writes in *Psychology of the Masses*,[82] and as Lacan teaches in *Seminar 9*,[83] the "ideal" is made in such a way that it can never be attained. In other words, no woman, however good, beautiful and sweet she may be, will escape the criticism (or self-criticism) of not reaching the ideal. One wonders how it is possible that, if we are talking about politics and criminal law, the discussion comes to revolve around issues such as the way someone speaks, the clothes she wears, or the accessories she uses. It seems that if that someone is a woman – and, even more so, if that woman does not adhere to the stereotype – she can be attacked on any of these grounds. Because, as feminism has taught us, the capitalist-patriarchal system has historically understood women as slaves; it has not only forced them to give birth and raise children, but also to do so with love.[84] Women who dare to exceed this model and become interested in issues outside of childrearing and family, such as participating in politics, will be easily labeled as deviant and stigmatized. In other words, there is only one thing worse than a corrupt male politician: a corrupt female politician.[85]

---

79 Pronto (2021) ¿Qué dice el parte médico de Florencia Kirchner? Jun. 9, https://www.pro nto.com.ar/actualidad/2021/6/9/que-dice-el-parte-medico-de-florencia-kirchner-176 279.html.

80 Badaro, Máximo (2020) Cacerolas: Rebelión y Felicidad, *Anfibia*, http://www.revistaanfi bia.com/cronica/cacerolas-rebelion-y-felicidad/.

81 ELA (2012) La tapa de Noticias y la violencia mediática, https://www.ela.org.ar/a2 /index.cfm?muestra&codcontenido=1237&plcontampl=12&aplicacion=app187&cnl =79&opc=50.

82 Freud, Sigmund. *Psicología de las masas y análisis del yo y otros textos.* Trad. Paulo César de Souza. En: Freud, Sigmund. *Obras completas.* Vol. 15, São Paulo: Companhia das Letras.

83 Lacan, Jacques. A ... (*op. cit.*).

84 Federici, Silvia, *Calibán y la Bruja*, Traficantes de Sueños, 1998.

85 On all this, see, for example, Azar, Indiana Rocío; Tavares Da Motta, Luiza. *La vio- lencia de género en el lawfare: un análisis de los casos de Dilma Rousseff y Cristina Fernández de Kirchner.* En: Aguilar Viana, Ana Cristina [ed.] Investigación, Género y Diversidad: Memorias de las III Jornadas de Investigación por/de/sobre las Mujeres. Vol. I. pp. 269–271; D'Adamo, Orland [et. al.]. *Mujeres Candidatas: Percepción Pública del Liderazgo Femenino.* En: Revista de Psicología Social, v. 23, n. 1. 2008; Pérez S; Aymá, A. *Medios, Multimodalidad, Género y Política: Cristina Fernández de Kirchner en Noticias.*

Added to this is the notion of intersectionality that explains how selectivity in terms of gender multiplies when it intersects with other aspects such as skin color, ethnicity or social status. In the case of Milagro Sala, detained in the province of Jujuy since January 16, 2016, the drop-by-drop persecution not only included evidentiary flaws, abuse of pretrial detention and violation of due process, but also the violation of the division of powers, a basic component of the democratic system. This occurred when the governor of the province of Jujuy urged his legislative majority to pass a law expanding the number of members of the highest provincial court and then appointed to the new positions on the court those same partisan deputies who had voted for the law, many of them relatives of the governor himself. In the criminal cases against Milagro Sala, witnesses proposed by the defense were systematically rejected, recusals of judges were denied "in limine" without justification and then the defense attorneys were sanctioned for raising them, the defense was deprived of the right to present evidence, benefits were given to detainees in other cases in order to implicate Sala as instigator years after the facts, preventive detention was ordered without basis in procedural risks, and new facts were imputed to her as instigator even when they occurred while she was already deprived of her liberty. The pending question is whether this massive violation of procedural guarantees would be tolerated by the citizenry and the political arc if Milagro were not an indigenous and poor woman, the perfect example of intersectionality.

Let us return to the analysis of this (intersectionally) selective judicial power that guarantees neliberal governability under the argument of the fight against corruption. What, then, is the limit of judicial intervention in politics? From the point of view of minimal legal rights,[86] the basic principle is respect for constitutional guarantees, including the balance of powers. This implies

En: Revista Observatorio. v. 3, n. 6. 2017. pp. 517–556. To understand how some of these political violences are especially linked to gender, c.e., v.g., PERFIL. *Clarín publicó el teléfono de la hija de Gils Carbó y ahora recibe amenazas.* Oct./2017. aveilable at: <https://www.perfil.com/noticias/politica/gils-carbo-dara-de-baja-el-celular-de-su-hija-porque-cla rin-lo-hizo-publico.phtml>. .date of access 12/12/2021; READY. ¿Qué dice el parte médico de Florencia Kirchner? Junio/2021. Aveilable at: <https://www.pronto.com.ar/act ualidad/2021/6/9/que-dice-el-parte-medico-de-florencia-kirchner-176279.html>. date of access 12/12/2021; BADARÓ, Maximo. Cacerolas: Rebelión y Felicidad. Anfibios. Available at: <https://www.revistaanfibia.com/cacerolas-rebelion-y-felicidad/>. date of access 12/12/2021; ELA. La tapa de Noticias y la violencia mediática. 2012. Aveilable at: <https://www.ela.org.ar/a2/index.cfm?muestra&codcontenido=1237&plcontampl=12&aplicacion=app 187&cnl=79&opc=50>. 2/12/2021.
86 Zaffaroni, Raúl (2018) Milagro, *Página/12*, Ago. 7.

that punitivity must be the last bastion of the rule of law to address conflicts. It cannot be used as a wild card when the electoral outcome or government decisions are displeasing to someone.

In other words, the judiciary cannot disrupt, undermine, override or cancel parliamentary decisions or a presidential election except in a situation of extreme constitutional gravity.[87] However, lawfare shows that, in open contradiction of this tenet, within the media-criminal-political system, the first two (media and judicial) are being used not to make the third (politics) transparent and fight corruption, but rather to govern outside democratic lines, going so far as to overrule decisions made by bodies directly elected by the people. Moreover, it does so with a redoubling of criminal selectivity that more boldly stigmatizes and over-criminalizes women, the poor and those of color. However, on a more optimistic note, attention to lawfare could still serve to open the debate and reverse the structural injustices of the penal systems that have accompanied us since the dawn of modernity.

14 Punitivism and Lawfare: The "More Punishment" Trap and the Irreparable Damage of Punitivity

Continuing with the need to limit punitivity while ensuring maximum respect for constitutional guarantees, it should be noted that the penal system cannot be used to curb the illegitimate over-criminalization of popular leaders nor to reverse the under-criminalization of social damage perpetrated by leaders aligned with the neoliberal agenda. Otherwise, there is a risk of falling into a circle of punishment in which the response to over-criminalization is more and more punishment, until there is no one left to lock the prison door because all of us would be inside.

In this sense, it should be noted that while the emphasis is on criminal law and individual retribution, the interests at stake may be different. What are those interests? Returning to the example of ordinary crime, one notes that police presence rarely makes neighborhoods more secure, and that imprisonment does not ensure the rehabilitation and resocialization of the person charged. The use of punitivity against marginalized populations avails itself of the discourse of security when its actions are in fact focused on the social control of marginalized sectors of the population. When we extend the

---

87   Ferrajoli, Luigi (2001) *Derecho y Razón*, Madrid: Trotta; Zaffaroni, Raúl, Alagia, Alejandro y Slokar, Alejandro (2002) Derecho Penal, op cit.

analysis to lawfare by over-criminalization, it becomes evident that punitivity is not capable of addressing complex, entrenched and global problems such as corruption. Its interests lie elsewhere, in extra-legal ends which, as previously mentioned, constitute strategies of governance over the persons charged and operate as a sword of Damocles over a whole sector of the political arc. Moreover, the judicialization of politics runs the risk of delegitimizing politics as a tool for transformation by spreading the perception that "all politicians are corrupt" or that "businessmen can do a better job," in line with the agenda of the Global North.

Added to all this is the fact that, even apart from this critical geopolitical perspective, punitivity rarely succeeds in effectively resolving conflicts. Following the lessons of penal abolitionism,[88] it is clear that even in minor crimes against property such as cell phone theft, in the best case scenario, those charged are subjected to a criminal process that will leave them in worse conditions to enter the labor market because they now have a criminal record, the trial will be paid for by the taxpayers, and the person affected by the theft will have to go to court to testify and will only receive his or her cell phone once the expertise and the process allow it. In "successfully" solved corruption cases, the scenario also shows a person charged, while the ill-gotten assets are hardly ever recovered, and the state-corporate structure that makes corruption possible remains intact.

The reduction of structural social problems to individual accusations is an intrinsic characteristic of criminal law. Mahmood Mamdani has shown how even in the most serious conceivable crimes, criminal law leaves the political project and the very violence of the state unchallenged.[89] Similarly, Ingrid Samset argues that criminal law focuses on individuals and actions between individuals, detached from the context of the norms, practices and conditions in which they act.[90] Thus, even in the most painful crimes, such as gender-based violence, feminist abolitionism calls for a focus not on convicting violent individuals, but on abolishing the conditions that make gender-based violence possible in the first place. In relation to lawfare, these reflections create a space for debating the real solutions to corruption. If we really want to solve the structural problems of a lack of transparency and the concentration of powers, the civil route and the seizure of assets, as well as preventive and structural

---

88   Hulsman, Louk (2000) "El enfoque abolicionista: Políticas criminales alternativas" en AAVV, *Criminología crítica y control social. El poder punitivo del Estado*, Rosario, Juris.

89   Mamdani, Mahmood (2020) Neither Settler nor Native. *The Making and Unmaking of Permanent Minorities*, Harvard University Press.

90   Samset, Ingrid (2020) International Journal of Transitional Justice, 14, 596–607.

control mechanisms, would seem to provide more promising paths to finding fundamental solutions.

In short, up to this point we have clarified that the penal system must be limited to ensure respect for the constitutional guarantees that are essential to the democratic system, that its application pursues extra-legal effects linked to specific interests and that, even if we were not critical of its use, punitivity can hardly go beyond individual solutions and address structural problems such as corruption. But to all this we must add another essential element: the use of punitivity is *irreparable*. A person deprived of his or her liberty who is later acquitted cannot recover that time of detention and the physical and emotional damage it involved. With lawfare, this irreparable damage not only affects the individual but the entire citizenry. Perhaps Lula's case is the best evidence of this: the Federal Supreme Court annulled all the sentences against him due to lack of proper jurisdiction,[91] and not only were the proceedings closed, but Lula was also permitted to run again in elections. However, this sentence was declared after he had already been branded before the people as corrupt, imprisoned, and deprived of competing electorally in the 2018 elections. Can we then say that with the ruling of the Federal Supreme Court, the fight against lawfare in Brazil has been won?

There are three irreparable effects that a judicial sentence cannot reverse. First, there is the damage to individual life, the time in prison, the suffering in the face of uncertainty, the experiences of which he was deprived (including, for Lula, the funerals of his brother and his grandson).[92] This damage to individual life is perhaps even more palpable in the accusations of the Argentine jurisdiction against former Foreign Minister Héctor Timmerman, who, in the framework of a lawfare case for over-criminalization, was prevented from traveling to the United States to undergo treatment for the cancer that eventually killed him.[93] Secondly, being socially labeled as "corrupt" is also irreparable. Once the media-judicial structure of the drop-by-drop coup fixes this idea in the minds of the citizenry, it is difficult for an intelligible sentence issued years after the fact to reverse the social image created. This discrediting of progressive politics transcends the figure of Lula and affects the democratic quality

91   TSF (2021) Supremo Tribunal Federal confirma anulação do julgamento que condenou Lula da Silva, Abr. 15, https://www.tsf.pt/mundo/supremo-tribunal-federal-confirma-anulacao-do-julgamento-que-condenou-lula-da-silva-13576509.html.

92   Pignotti, Dario (2019) Lula llora la muerte de su nieto Arthur, *Página/12*, Mar. 2, https://www.pagina12.com.ar/178142-lula-llora-la-muerte-de-su-nieto-arthur.

93   Kollman, Raúl (2018) Con desprecio a la razón humanitaria, *Página/12*, Ene. 10, https://www.pagina12.com.ar/88154-con-desprecio-a-la-razon-humanitaria.

of the country. Finally, the irreparability is evident in the electoral field. The over-criminalization of Lula removed him from the elections, altered the democratic game, and made possible the election of the opponent Jair Bolsonaro. The nullity of the sentences against him cannot give Lula back the possibility of participating in the electoral process or repair the damage caused to the citizenry by Bolsonaro's management, including denialist policies of the pandemic that caused hundreds of thousands of deaths and that could be qualified as an international criminal offense.[94] Faced with this situation, the only question is: what to do?

15   What to Do about Lawfare? Towards a Popular Precautionary Criminology

Given the irreparable nature of the punitivity's actions, the measures that can be adopted by the judicial powers are essential, but not sufficient. Even the most efficient criminal justice system requires time to process cases, and this alone may cause the aforementioned irreparable damage at the three levels described above. In other words, the solution to lawfare cannot come only from legal struggle and judicial reform, because the law arrives late, after democracy has already been manipulated, after the leaders have already been labeled corrupt and their individual lives damaged. This is the inevitable consequence of a justice system that can only act on individuals and not enact structural changes, that intervenes a posteriori and not preventively, and that operates from courts and with mechanisms and language disconnected from the citizenry.

At the same time, in the neighborhoods and within social organizations, the people themselves can confront the slow drip of violence. A key example in Argentina was the so-called "2 for 1" movement.[95] The Supreme Court issued a ruling that privileged the reduction of sentences for people accused of crimes against humanity, and a mobilized citizenry did not wait for national or Inter-American judicial mechanisms to reverse the sentence, or even for the other branches of government to intervene. This, as noted so far, in the best of cases would only have happened after a certain period of time, when the accused would probably have already enjoyed the freedom granted to them. Instead the mobilized people took to the streets immediately and managed *to prevent*

---

94   Idoeta, Paula Adamo (2021) Bolsonaro pode ser julgado em Haia por gestão da pandemia?, BBC, Jun. 26, https://www.bbc.com/portuguese/brasil-57576293.

95   https://www.bbc.com/mundo/noticias-america-latina-39876510.

the implementation of the sentence and, at the same time, to create the conditions for the institutional reversal of the state of affairs through the enactment of a law with general effects for all defendants in similar conditions.

With lawfare it is more complicated because it is not easy to understand the course of the cases (what the cases are about, when the decisions are legitimate and when they are not, in which cases constitutional guarantees are violated and in which ones the rule of law is respected). Nor are there any civil society organizations specifically dedicated to the fight against lawfare. The proposal to reverse these challenges is, however, more justified: to create and consolidate, via social movements, a "popular legal culture." Popular legal culture would consist, first of all, in incorporating the functions of justice into the agenda for social transformation. Secondly, it would disseminate basic legal knowledge to smash the ivory tower in which the courts find themselves, facilitating a civic control that would prevent the cases of lawfare by over-criminalization from advancing. Training is necessary for this purpose. This can take place through events that bring the law closer to social movements and make it understandable, alternative media and social networks that incorporate court news so that the only voice is not that of the hegemonic media, and mechanisms for disseminating information about lawfare prosecutors, defenders and judges to reveal their actions and shatter as well the protection of anonymity.[96]

The creation of this popular legal culture would also involve dialogue with the university, in a multidimensional process including greater decentralization and accessibility of the faculties so that more people and more organizations can have access (as shown in Argentina, the example of the opening of universities in the greater Buenos Aires region),[97] research and training programs shared between the university and organizations in the neighborhoods in informal processes of democratization of knowledge (as in the case of popular university projects), and the involvement of social organizations to nurture curricula, academic tools and university faculty.

Education and research at the service of concrete social needs and problems is fundamental to checking lawfare. Fake news and media manipulation could be reversed with reliable and clear data from qualitative and quantitative

96   Vegh Weis, Valeria (2021b) Para derrumbar el lawfare, la pelea es desde abajo, *El Destape*, Mayo 7, https://www.eldestapeweb.com/opinion/lawfare/para-derrumbar-el-lawfare-la-pelea-es-desde-abajo-2021575025.

97   Centro de Estudios de Educación Argentina (2018) Las Nuevas Universidades del Conurbano Bonaerense, http://repositorio.ub.edu.ar/bitstream/handle/123456789/8694/ceaagosto2018.pdf?sequence=1&isAllowed=y.

studies on ongoing cases and media-judicial actions, including who are the defendants, who are those who file the cases, what rules are applied, how long it takes to resolve the cases, what is the role of gender, class and ethnicity, who are behind the parties involved, and even what the interests are at stake.

Likewise, a brotherhood between universities and social movements could open up opportunities for a greater development of alternative media committed to the promotion of popular legal culture. This does not neglect the essential need to de-monopolize the existing media. In the Argentine experience, this is a fight against windmills, but knowing that media concentration and its partisan use constitute a regional problem (with media corporations operating in several countries), is it not time for a regional strategy to ensure plurality of voices and thoughts in the media?

Finally, lawfare indicates as indispensable (although not sufficient) the need for judicial reform. In this sense, lawfare opens the door to changes that would not only reverse this phenomenon, but might even help to limit the mechanisms of selectivity in general and ensure greater respect for the rights of all persons subject to the criminal justice system. A reform with this scope would include intersectionality, interdisciplinarity and transparency as its basis.

The federal judiciary that resolves lawfare cases in Argentina today only has 30% of its decision-making positions occupied by women, while the heads of the Public Prosecutor's Office in the 24 provinces of the country are all men.[98] Seeking to disarm these inequities, intersectionality involves structural transformations in terms of gender equity, but also in terms of class and skin color to ensure equal participation in decision-making positions with a view to "making justice look like the society it represents."[99] While it should be noted that the mere condition of being women, indigenous or trans does not guarantee a specific sensitivity to lawfare or social issues in general, it is essential in terms of ensuring equality. In fact, according to the results of some research, greater gender diversity seems to have an impact on jurisdictional decisions that are more respectful of the rule of law.[100] In any case, for intersectionality to materialize in the concrete actions of justice, the equitable distribution of positions must be complemented with comprehensive, mandatory and critical training in the content of written exams in competitive examinations and personal

---

98   Soria, Martín (2021) *Conversatorio: ¿Cómo incorporar la perspectiva de género en el Poder Judicial?* https://www.youtube.com/watch?v=9mTA7gfOjOM.

99   Gómez Alcorta, Eli (2021) Del Lawfare a una Reforma Judicial Feminista y Popular, *Movemos,* Mar. 30.

100   Songer, Donald R y Crews-Meyer, Kelley A.(2000) "Does Judge Gender Matter? Decision Making in State Supreme Courts," *Social Science Quarterly,* v. 81, n. 3, pp. 750–762.

interviews, in the curricular training to be evaluated, in the form of mandatory courses prior to taking office and as a condition for continuity in the position.

A task as complex as that of disarming lawfare can hardly be done within the legal system. As noted, the judiciary issues its decisions in writing, using incomprehensible jargon and without any accountability. Interdisciplinary teams could make room for the inclusion of communicators so that magistrates can make the results of their actions and decisions known to the people involved in an understandable language. The adoption of clear and simple language with short sentences can be nourished by concrete experiences such as those provided by the Arriola decision of the former Supreme Court, or the lessons of Judge Mario Juliano.[101] Moreover, it is worth asking whether the inclusion of other disciplines could lead to the possibility that what today are conceived as privileges of judicial employment exclusive to the sector (stability, salary, earnings, vacations) could be re-conceived as rights that could lead to better conditions in other professions.

Interdisciplinary approaches would incorporate direct online and face-to-face communication channels where specialized journalists and the same actors of the judiciary, as well as interested citizens, could learn about the content of judicial decisions, at least those of public importance. In other words, the accessibility mechanisms present in the executive branch could be replicated in the judiciary, through which the heads of state and ministers explain the content of their decrees and most relevant decisions to the public. In a remarkable example of the exception that should be the rule, Cristina Fernández de Kirchner used the public hearings in the framework of the criminal proceedings against her to provide a message in simple language not only to the magistrates, but also to the citizens.[102] Proving that there is no lack of interest, more than 20,000 people watched the hearing live and hundreds of thousands of others on tape. Beyond the specific cases, these hearings opened the way to think of technology and orality as a bridge between justice and ordinary people. Other changes could include a friendly web page of the justice system so that users can know the faces of the magistrates, their CVs, and information about their training, along with links to access the hearings.

Finally, simple, conversational, accessible language could pave the way for transparency and accountability as a shield to avoid the systematic violation of constitutional guarantees so dear to lawfare. In this sense, any reform must involve changes in transparency. This would involve banishing papers (as

---

101   Fallo Arriola (A. 891. XLIV); Obra de Mario Juliano, http://www.pensamientopenal.com
        .ar/autores/mario-alberto-juliano.
102   Ver https://www.youtube.com/watch?v=F55YCVDxhtI.

opposed to in-person meetings), notifications (as opposed to dialogues), and delegation of functions (as opposed to personalization). The current composition of prosecutors' offices, courts and public defenders' offices is a stumbling block to this path of orality and transparency. For each judge, prosecutor or defender, there are twenty employees who are the ones who really know the details of the case, to the point that they even take statements from the accused and the victims. Could a judicial reform break with this feudal scheme and spread the multiplication of dependencies so that each magistrate is solely responsible for his or her cases, with a minimum administrative support? Can we even imagine a decentralized justice service in which the courts are located in the neighborhoods and the neighbors can directly access them?[103]

This bridge with the citizenry as a springboard for transparency and a shield against the violation of guarantees would need to be complemented with monitoring. At present we do not know what the criteria of the magistrates is for rejecting or requesting jurisdiction in a case, or how they choose the order in which the cases in process are resolved. Could a judicial reform introduce a monitoring system through a civil society observatory, such as the one currently carried out by the Permanent Assembly for Human Rights and the Center for Legal and Social Studies regarding appointments and promotions based on the involvement in State terrorism?[104] The civic control of social and civil society organizations could then contribute to transparency while at the same time promoting the development of a popular legal culture.[105]

Finally, from within social movements, universities, mass media and the justice system, lawfare can be curbed by better recognizing the rights of those who cannot exercise them, and by requiring a greater transparency from those who enjoy privileges. It is a matter of developing a "popular precautionary criminology" that can preventively identify when, under the guise of the fight against corruption, punitivity is used as a governance strategy to discipline the leaders of our region and undermine much-needed social justice agendas.

When the response of punitivity is so aggressive that a criminal case puts democratic continuity at risk, perhaps we are no longer faced with an act of

---

103   Vegh Weis, Valeria (2019) Algunas Notas para Reflexionar sobre el Modelo de Cortes Comunitarias en los Estados Unidos, en Fava, Gabriel y Alonso, Silvina. (eds.) *Nuevas Dimensiones del Principio de Legalidad en el Proceso Penal. Justicia Restaurativa,* Buenos Aires: Rubinzal.

104   CELS (2016) *Derechos humanos y control civil de las fuerzas armadas,* Buenos Aires, CELS.

105   Vegh Weis, Valeria (2021c) Criminologías y Géneros. Por una Reforma Judicial Feminista y Antipunitivista, en Red de Profesoras de Derecho Penal (eds.) *Reforma Judicial Feminista,* Buenos Aires: Editores del Sur.

justice, but quite the opposite. We have repeated it insistently, but less us be perfectly clear: punitivity has always been dangerous and has never solved anything. There is a great risk that unproven accusations will end up operating like a sword of Damocles, especially against those who do not bow to the determinations of global political-financial power.

Knowing that this is a regional problem and that there is no room in the local judiciary, at least for the moment, to put these political-media strategies on the dock, several ideas have been floated about. Based on experiences such as the Russell Tribunal, which judged the U.S. intervention in Vietnam, and the popular trials against civil accomplices carried out by the *Mothers of Plaza de Mayo Association*, the creation of an ethical tribunal against lawfare has been proposed.[106] The project aims to judge the irregularity and illegality of this mechanism and to raise awareness of its function of social domination. The debate has only just begun.

---

106   https://www.eldestapeweb.com/nota/el-tribunal-etico-de-juzgamiento-del-lawfare
      --202011717500.

CHAPTER 4

Some Exemplary Lawfare Cases

Cristina Caamaño, Eugenio Raúl Zaffaroni and Valeria Vegh Weis

1   A First Case of Wiretapping for "Shameful Law of Criminal Procedure"

The story begins with a triple homicide that took place in Buenos Aires in 2008. In addition to those convicted of the crime, a man who remained a fugitive from federal justice for several years was also accused. The grisly event was connected to the illegal trafficking of ephedrine.

Several years later, Graciela Ocaña, a member of the alliance which would later back Mauricio Macri when he ran for president, filed a criminal complaint against Oscar Parrilli, head of the Federal Intelligence Agency, alleging that he protected or covered up the fugitive. A new stage of "shameful Law of criminal procedure" was about to commence, and it was deemed advantageous to suggest a relationship between drug trafficking and the political party to which Parrilli belonged, at that time the one in power. The result of the elections was not enough: "shameful Law of criminal procedure" always does what it can to expose its so-called "despicable," "horrible," and "corrupt" political adversaries, even if they are not involved in any open cases. How so? Recall this special form of procedural law has at its disposal a means of affecting third parties (colleagues, family members, friends, the denunciator's grocer): wiretapping. Who else will be exposed? The grocer? No, no *mass media* outlet is going to put up with so many hours just for that. They are going for more, for the person with the most influence in Parrilli's political movement in order to reaffirm that figure as the archetype of horror.

So it was that we all found ourselves spending countless hours watching prime time TV and reading endless pages of private dialogues between Oscar Parrilli and the outgoing president Cristina Fernández de Kirchner, neither of whom, by then, any longer held office. Did these dialogues confirm Parrilli's criminal activity? No. Did they include any information whatsoever about the location of the fugitive involved in the 2008 homicide? No, nor did it matter because by then the fugitive was already in custody. So they were wiretapping the conversations of a presumed accomplice of a fugitive who had already been caught and was now in custody of the police? Yes, and with a court order to do so. Proceduralists of "true Law of criminal procedure" would say that they were fishing for something. But "shameful Law of criminal procedure" does not simply take its fishing pole out into the open river and wait for criminal activities to come nibble; it specifically fishes for private conversations between certain people that will help establish those people as the source of all evil.

Eventually a number of dialogues in the voices of Parrilli and Fernandez were publicly exposed, demonstrating that the outgoing president called her former colleague an "asshole" (*pelotudo*), that she is not very lady-like, basically whatever it takes to show that she is "bad," "very bad" (a mortal sin for a woman), because in another private chat with her friend she refers to another politician as a "fat son of a bitch" or says that some people should not get so "butt-hurt," or mentions that both of them used to talk about politics every day (and how dare they do so if they have already left their positions and should never hold public office again!?), or that in private she talks about other people in politics (and you don't talk on the phone about people who are not present!).

All this happened bit by bit, over the course of several months, during which time "shameful Law of criminal procedure" gradually took over without anybody stopping it. And what did this wiretapping reveal? Well, the fugitive was in custody. The accused Parrilli talked on the phone a lot with his former boss and had nothing to do with it. Did Cristina Fernández de Kirchner? No, but we all got to listen in on her clearly private conversations thanks to this flexible procedural tool. Note that this whole case occurred after the Supreme Court took over the "wiretapping" thanks to Mauricio Macri's creation of DAJUDECO, as discussed in Chapter.

2   Another Case of Eavesdropping: Santiago and Sergio Maldonado

Another interesting case to analyze is that of the young Santiago Maldonado, who on August 1, 2017 was participating in an indigenous community demonstration in Cushamen, in the Argentine province of Chubut. We know that there was a violent dispersal executed mainly by agents of the National Gendarmerie under the command of Minister Patricia Bullrich, and that that same day, Santiago's disappearance was noticed by his Mapuche companions, who declared him missing. Sadly his lifeless body was found on October 17 of that year, a few meters from where he had last been seen.

There are many details that we will not be able to include here, but, considering the statements made by political officials and the ways in which the mass media represented the event, it is impossible to ignore a concerted effort to present this young man in a negative light, primarily because he was a protestor who belonged to a people who have been suffering inequalities for five hundred years and who were seeking recognition of their rights over lands that belong to them, but which have been deemed too beautiful to be anything other than summer vacation resorts.

And here "shameful Law of criminal procedure" comes into play. Whom could they spy on if Santiago was no longer around? His family. A wiretapping was ordered for Sergio Maldonado, Santiago's brother. Was he suspected for playing a role in his brother's death? No. Was he hiding any information related to that death? No. It was simply a question of looking for some material that would expose him as another one of those "despicable" beings that Santiago sought to defend, "all of them violent liars."

This is how Sergio Maldonado's private conversations reached the mainstream media, thanks to "shameful Law of criminal procedure." All of this took place shortly after Mauricio Macri had established the new Supreme Court wiretapping office. Leaks again? Yes, unfortunately "shameful Law of criminal procedure" is indifferent as to whether we are dealing with the victim of state violence or his family. There was a court order to wiretap Sergio Maldonado: the strange thing – well, not really so strange – is that the judge never asked Sergio to make an official statement, with the obligatory oath to tell the truth imposed by law, but instead preferred to hear from him in this striking way.

The judge who then took over the investigation nullified the wiretapping order. However, a subsequent ruling rendered this nullity null and void, and at the time of writing, this case has yet to be definitively decided by the Supreme Court, which formally still forms a part of DAJUDECO, the source of all these private conversations that "shameful Law of criminal procedure" continues to exploit.

The same Law of criminal procedure has yet to saddle anyone with the responsibility for Santiago's death.[1]

3   The Imprisonment of Political Opponents: More on the "Irurzun
       Doctrine"

In 2017, as part of the case identified as "Larregina, Miguel A. and Others w/ o Detention," the majority faction of the Federal Criminal and Correctional Chamber revoked the decision that had allowed then-Congressman Julio De

---

1   https://www.cels.org.ar/web/2018/06/caso-maldonado-pedimos-que-se-confirme-la-nuli
    dad-de-las-escuchas-y-se-investiguen-las-filtraciones/; Página de Santiago Maldonado:
    http://www.santiagomal-donado.com/archivo-de-noticias/.

Vido to remain free during the proceedings against him, and ordered his arrest, pending his impeachment.

First, Judge Martín Irurzun ruled that the freedom of the accused threatened to obstruct the investigation of the case. Taking into account that the investigation entailed allegations of complex acts of corruption, which would have involved officials from different offices of the State acting together under the protection of its structure, it was decided that to properly examine the procedural risks, the analysis should not be limited to personal histories or to how the witnesses and accused behaved during the trial.

The argument for detaining Congressman De Vido before his trial, was premised on alleged "functional ties woven together under the cover of a criminal agreement," i.e. secret criminal connections that, it was dogmatically asserted, continued to exist and which might serve to obstruct the investigation.

Curiously enough, in an act of circular reasoning, the accusation itself was used as the guideline to evaluate the risk of the investigation being hindered. The ruling invoked charges that, at that point in the trial, had not yet been proven: "At this stage, and always presumably, it is not feasible to distance De Vido from the scenario described here, since he has been accused by the prosecutor [...] of playing a leading role in the events currently under investigation."

Report 86/09 of the Inter-American Commission on Human Rights, among many other documents, insists that the procedural risk of flight or obstruction of investigation must be based on objective circumstances. And yet this idea that former officials under investigation for alleged acts of corruption retain a residual power that would somehow allow them to flee or hinder the investigation was affirmed, and without any objective basis whatsoever. To paraphrase the Italian jurist Danilo Zolo, this could be considered another example of "Conqueror's Justice."

Historically, pretrial detention has functioned to legitimize the use of punitivity against the most vulnerable members of society. Lately, it has found another use: to punish the politically vanquished. Disciplining by means of criminal law is not new, and perhaps this is why our colleague Raúl Zaffaroni has affirmed that pretrial detention constitutes "the squaring of the circle."

And while it is true that, at some point, we are faced with an unsolvable problem because there is no doubt that, in the face of particularly serious criminal acts with abundant evidence, the impossibility of trial and firm conviction in the immediate future will leave no alternative but to resort to preventive imprisonment, we must not fail to recognize that anticipatory punishment must remain the exception. The vast majority of cases, on the other hand, find a solution in legal theory. Judges might then use it as a last resort, without fear, without pressure of any kind, and with a firm understanding of criminal law as that which serves to limit the punitivity of the State.

4   The Memorandum with Iran

If he were ever resurrected in Argentina, Poor Baron Montesquieu would lie right down and die again. He is the French jurist who, in 1700, first proposed to divide government power into the executive, legislative, and judicial branches, with a system of control shared among the three, but with each always respecting the other two branches. Recently in Argentina this idea was abandoned when the judiciary chose to criminalize a decision that had been voted on by Congress.

The Memorandum with Iran was an agreement signed by Argentina and that country. Its purpose was to facilitate the investigation of the AMIA bombing, a 1994 attack on the Asociación Mutual Israelita Argentina that left 85 dead and 300 injured. It was a memorandum of understanding voted and approved by the Congress of the Nation, but it was never passed into law because it was declared unconstitutional by the Federal Chamber of Criminal Cassation.

Although it was approved by Congress in accordance with the methods specified by the Constitution, and although it never actually passed into law, the whole process involving the signing of the agreement was declared criminal. Specifically, on January 14, 2015, the federal prosecutor Alberto Nisman denounced before the judge investigating the AMIA cover-up case President Cristina Fernández de Kirchner and former Foreign Minister Héctor Timerman, among others.

After Nisman's death, and after the Federal Chamber established jurisdiction, the prosecutor Gerardo Pollicita took over the case. The accusations he made during the preliminary investigation request were based on the fact that the highest authorities within the Executive Power (the then-President and Foreign Minister Héctor Timerman) "would have developed actions with the authority to exculpate the Iranians identified as responsible for the AMIA bombing so that they could be removed from the action of justice." The maneuver, Pollicita claimed, would have been carried out with the help of other persons of that political party, and would have been achieved by means of the memorandum. With this objective, according to the prosecution, the accused 1) would have tried to create an organization called "Truth Commission," with powers to assume strictly judicial functions that would replace the judge and prosecutor to whom the case legally corresponded, and 2) would have downgraded the red alert pertaining to the search for five of the people imputed in the AMIA case. Thus, the prosecutor accused them of treason and of concealing or hindering the investigation.

Judge Daniel Rafecas declared the case a confused muddle and dismissed the charges on the argument that it was unnecessary to consider if a crime had occurred because the memorandum never entered into law, meaning that the "Truth Commission" in question was never created. It would be like accusing someone of burning the chicken when someone else had already turned off the oven before it could even have started to cook. As for the lowering of the red alerts, there was no proof as to whether or not this act had been committed, nor would the then-President or Chancellor even have had the authority to do so: Interpol is a very complex international organization and does not answer to Argentine officials.[2]

Judge Rafecas's decision was confirmed by the Federal Chamber, but later reversed by the Chamber of Cassation, which reopened the case. And so, after having been dismissed on two fronts, the same accusation was made yet again, and with no investigation to back it up. Anyone could have called Interpol to ask if someone had requested that the alert level be lowered, but no one did. Ronald Noble, who was the head of Interpol at the time of the signing of the memorandum, was never asked to testify.

This became really serious when, sustaining the order of preventive detention without grounds to do so (as there was no danger of flight or of hindering the investigation), Judge Claudio Bonadio refused to release Timmerman, who was suffering from an aggressive cancer and required daily treatments. The prosecutor's office supported Timmerman's request to leave the country to try a treatment that could help him with his illness, but Bonadio rejected it. Timmerman died at his residence, still facing charges in this case.

5   The "Future Dollar" Case

The case was opened on October 30, 2015, when Representative Mario Negri and Senator Federico Pinedo pressed charges for fraudulent administration in response to the decision of the Central Bank of the Argentine Republic to arrange for the sale of American dollars at a price lower than the New York market for future sales. This would permit an investor to buy dollars in the domestic market and then sell them in the New York market for a speculative gain.

---

2   Resolution of Judge Rafecas, available at https://www.cij. gov.ar/nota-14965-El-juez-Rafecas-desestim--la-denuncia-presentada-por-el-fiscal-Nisman.html. Sobre este caso en particular, ver la serie de Netflix El fiscal, la presidenta y el espía, de Justin Webster.

Good or bad, this is a monetary policy decision made by the Central Bank. Not everything can be a crime! Judge Bonadio himself formally acknowledged the legitimacy of the Central Bank to intervene in the monetary stability of the country: "It is well known that national central banks play an important role in the foreign exchange markets; they attempt to control money supply, inflation, and interest rates, and they often have official or unofficial exchange rates, and use their often substantial foreign exchange reserves to stabilize the market." He continued: "It can therefore be affirmed that the future dollar operation is a legitimate mechanism used by the Central Bank to achieve one of its central purposes, namely, to promote monetary and/or exchange rate stability." Notwithstanding, he then explains that these operations must be carried out at the "market price" and that "this precisely what was not done," thereby justifying the criminal charge.

Who sits on the dock? Bonadio pointed his finger at Cristina Fernández de Kirchner, claiming that "a financial operation of this magnitude, in which in less than 45 working days, open positions in the Central Bank jumped from USD 5 billion to USD 17 billion, clearly unleashing immediate economic and political effects, could not possibly be carried out without the express approval from the highest economic and political decision-making level of the National Executive Power." By what legal argument did he claim that the former President could still be imputed for a decision that did not go through her? Bonadio availed himself of a theory put forth by the German jurist Claus Roxin, which allows persons who occupy the highest echelons of an organized power structure to be charged for crimes even if they did not directly commit them. This is a very sensitive legal tool that can be dangerous because it extends punitivity and detaches it from the commission of the act. For this reason, even Roxin himself states that this theory should exclusively be used in cases of crimes against humanity or of organized crime, such as those that occurred in Nazi Germany. It seems that Bonadio skipped that part of the text.

What happened to the people who bought future dollars? Here there emerged the possibility that the judge could say different things, depending on the "client." At the end of 2016, then-Deputy Chief of Cabinet Mario Quintana, then-Secretary of Public Policy Coordination Gustavo Lopetegui, and other officials belonging to the Mauricio Macri government were also denounced in the "future dollar" case. However, this time, Bonadio declared the crime to be "non-existent," arguing that "the conduct of those who bought future dollars after the Central Bank made such an appealing offer cannot be criminally reproached." The beneficiaries of future dollar purchases were acquitted in

June 2018. Among the buyers was Luis Caputo, later president of the Central Bank, who has not been heard from for some time.[3]

---

3 Processing is available in https://www.cij.gov.ar/nota-21450-El-juez-Bo¬nadio-proces--a -Cristina-Kirchner-en-la-causa-por-el-d-lar-futuro.html (specially p. 46 y 199).

First Afterword

Eli Gómez Alcorta

Even if you have already finished reading the book, it requires some regional contextualization.[1] It has already been explained that the abuse of criminal law as a means of governance is expanding in Latin America, and that in Argentina, not only was it used, but its abuse was also abused.

To situate this book and these abuses, we need to recount a little of the history of shameful judicial power.

While illegal repression was systematically carried out by the last civil-military dictatorship in our country, while people "disappeared," were kidnapped, tortured, and murdered and their babies and children appropriated, human rights organizations as well as the families of those victims sought answers from the judiciary. Relatives, mothers and grandmothers of the victims not only went to governmental offices, military offices, churches, hospitals, shelters, and children's homes, but also to courts throughout the country. Between 1976 and 1983, 8,335 *habeas corpus* petitions were filed, part of the urgent search for the whereabouts of thousands of people who had disappeared as a result of the actions of the terrorist state.

Those appeals, with few exceptions, were rejected, and some were even penalized with fines. Far from fulfilling their duty to investigate the fate of the detained and disappeared, the judiciary endorsed and reified the methodology of systematic illegal repression, and played a vital role in sustaining it.

The truth is that during the civil-military dictatorship, the actions of the members of the judiciary and the Public Prosecutor's Office did not simply obstruct access to justice in relation to these crimes; they oscillated between a "militant complicity" and a "banal complacency."

The de facto government found the judiciary no obstacle when it came to carrying out the most serious criminal acts of our recent history.

Only ten years after the return to democracy, in 1994, Argentina was shaken by the bombing of the AMIA/DAIA headquarters, the largest in our history.

At that time, the emblematic building of the Supreme Court was beginning to fill with judges and officials. In one of its offices, a judge arranged to pay one of the people accused in that attack USD 400,000 to lie in order to redirect the judicial investigation. The friends of the Federal Police helped

---

1 Human Rights Lawyer, UBA Professor and feminist.

twist the investigation of a friend of the then-President, and the Secretariat of Intelligence (SIDE, discussed in Chapter 2) tapped into its reserves to buy a false version of the facts, which would lead to many years in prison for several policemen who, though *non sancto*, were not involved in that event. This mafioso maneuver, which involved the highest authorities of the Executive Branch, the Federal Police, the Intelligence Agency, the judiciary, and the Public Prosecutor's Office, and which entailed kidnappings, torture, the persecution of witnesses, bribes, visits of judges to the prison, and informal interventions by perpetrators of genocides who at that time still enjoyed total immunity, took place within the context of a judicial case and during the era of democracy.

In those same halls that the victims and relatives of that attack still walked, the judiciary, members of the legislature, and the state intelligence agency, among others, were penning another dark page in the history of "shameful judicial power." To this day, no one knows how the attack happened, or who is responsible for it. Impunity is an open wound.

The authors of this book have explained the mechanisms used to dismember and destroy Law of criminal procedure, thereby converting criminal cases into strategies of governance. They have demonstrated that these mechanisms were used at different times, in different ways, by different judicial agents, hand in hand with other social and political actors, against different people; perhaps what is unique about our own era is the enormous synchronization and precision of this machinery deployed for such a marked political purpose.

For example, "shameful criminal law" is always the one used to criminalize indigenous peoples and their leaders. It criminalizes social protest and the exercise of individual rights by shifting the social conflict to the judicial sphere, decontextualizing community struggle, individualizing collective action and, as a consequence, depoliticizing social movements.

Shameful criminal law procedure is and has been common currency, not only in the Supreme Court, but throughout the length and breadth of our country. The essential function of "true criminal law" is to contain irrational punitivity and, as we know, it is wielded by the judiciary.

For there to be a "true criminal and criminal procedure law," the members of the judicial system must also be truthful. This book presents us with a warning: any political project that seeks to sustain and develop greater levels of democratization and social justice must necessarily assume the commitment to build new schemes for the administration of justice with social and democratic legitimacy, as part of its greater obligation to critical thought and emancipatory political practice.

We must dare to imagine a new relationship between the judiciary and democracy, and ask ourselves how the people might intervene in the administration of justice, what citizen participation ought to look like, what type of control and accountability would best guarantee the transparent and effective actions of the magistrates, how judges and prosecutors should be selected or removed in a democracy (perhaps by popular vote) and how long their terms should last, what institutional mechanisms should regulate judicial decision-making processes, how to establish a relative degree of autonomy without generating unjustified and unproductive privileges, how to prevent corporate practices, and how to better put the democratic exercise of judicial power at the service of the public, among many other questions.

In the constitution and structuring of the judiciary, and in the practices that derive therefrom, the dispute between a formal and a substantive democracy is fiercer than ever before. And in this sense, the continuation of judicial agencies as they are currently conceived promises us life in a very feeble democracy.

Second Afterword

Atilio Boron

After reading this book, I am gripped with the sensation of having made a journey through an ominous and threatening territory, whose dimensions and topography I knew only in a rudimentary way.[1] But then I think of another metaphor, perhaps happier than the previous one, though equally didactic. I knew of the marvelous works of art guarded in the Louvre, and as a visitor pressed for time, whenever I returned to Paris I would rush to contemplate with delight the *Venus de Milo, The Winged Victory of Samothrace, The Mona Lisa,* or Eugene Delacroix's *Liberty Leading the People.* But on one of those occasions I was lucky enough to be accompanied by a French friend, Pierre, a curator and connoisseur not only of the history of art but also of all the nooks and crannies of that immense museum, and the explanation he gave me was fascinating, almost a revelation. Not only of each of the works mentioned above but of many others too, as well as of the architectural details of that building, the exquisite illumination of each of the objects kept there, the care to which they are subjected, the work that goes on in the immense undergrounds of the palace, where an anonymous army of painters, sculptors and experts of all kinds make it possible for us to continue to enjoy those works centuries after their creation. I remember as if it were today how when I left the Louvre after such an extraordinary visit I was speechless. We left the museum without exchanging goodbyes, I was overwhelmed by the phenomenal wealth that I had been able to contemplate for the first time in all its magnitude thanks to my providential guide. Pierre respected my silence and like a couple of zombies we headed towards the Rue de Rivoli to find a bar where we could recuperate from the very long walk inside the museum and process everything we had seen. We stumbled upon the Café Marly and it was only when we were able to sit down at one of the tiny tables set up in the *trottoir* that I recovered my ability to speak and could begin to sort through the chaos of sensations in my head, bombarding Pierre with an endless number of questions and increasingly specific inquiries about the *Mona Lisa,* the Delacroix painting, and what we had seen earlier that day.

I share this anecdote because something similar happened to me while reading this magnificent book. As a political scientist I was well aware that in

---

1 Senior Researcher at CONICET.

the last fifteen or twenty years, a novel and aberrant phenomenon had made its appearance in Latin America, a new political pathology had been added to the many others that plague our history: *lawfare*. The signs were unquestionable and, moreover, as time went by, this malicious manipulation of the law to serve spurious interests became more and more frequent. Equally irrefutable was the genesis of the disease: the change in the strategy and tactics of the White House to regain total control of the countries south of the Rio Bravo by destabilizing or overthrowing governments unwilling to submit to its mandates. If, up until the Malvinas Argentinas War, Washington relied entirely on the efficacy of the armed forces to overthrow disaffected governments, after the traumatic experience of that war there was a radical turnaround. The atrocities committed by U.S.-sponsored dictatorships unleashed a generalized repudiation and a growing anti-American sentiment which, with the election of Hugo Chávez in Venezuela, took on worrisome proportions for the White House. To make matters worse, the change that took place in Venezuela unleashed a "domino effect." The Venezuelan victory was followed by the electoral triumphs of Lula da Silva in Brazil, Néstor Kirchner in Argentina, Tabaré Vázquez in Uruguay, Evo Morales in Bolivia, Manuel Zelaya in Honduras, Rafael Correa in Ecuador, Cristina Fernández de Kirchner in Argentina, and Fernando Lugo in Paraguay, and this unsettling trend convinced the "US-American" strategists of the need to devise alternative, less tricky and above all less visible ways to achieve what was previously achieved by means of military coups.

In tune with the new strategy, the failed coup d'état against Hugo Chávez in 2002 was surrounded by legal paraphernalia that worked to conceal the existence of flagrant constitutional violations. The Supreme Court issued a ruling denying the existence of a coup d'état and acknowledging that what had occurred was a curious "power vacuum" (since Chávez no longer exercised presidential functions), and that the new President, Pedro Carmona Estanga, had patriotically helped put an end to such dangerous situation. The same would happen later with the failed attempts to overthrow Evo Morales in 2008 (including the partition of Bolivia) and Rafael Correa in September 2010. But the imperialists did not relent, and they did score several triumphs: the "institutionally" ousting (read: "soft coups") of Mel Zelaya in 2009, Fernando Lugo in 2012, and Dilma Rousseff in 2016. The South American socio-political picture is changing rapidly, aggravated by the defeat of Kirchnerism in the presidential elections of 2015 (which gave renewed impetus to the onslaught against Dilma) and, more recently, the absurd defeat of the Frente Amplio in Uruguay before a reactionary coalition in which, together with the decrepit traditional parties, a party of those nostalgic for the dictatorship and the era of torture all joined forces. The triumphs of Andrés Manuel López Obrador in

Mexico and Alberto Fernández in Argentina are encouraging signs, but they face unprecedented and formidable challenges, with the fatal combination of the pandemic and the deep economic crises affecting almost every economy in the world now added to the illegitimate foreign debt. More recently, the "classic coup" staged by a racist and neo-colonial minority against Evo Morales in Bolivia shows that Washington does not adhere to any principles, and that if the institutional mechanisms do not allow it to put on a farce of "impeachment" or to manipulate the electoral results, it is ready to reintroduce into the political scene a repressive apparatus (which the United States trains, finances and arms) in order to overthrow a legitimate president. It will even commit flagrant violations of international legality and designate a monkey like Juan Guaidó as "president in charge" of the Bolivarian Republic of Venezuela, with the infamous complicity of the European Union.

The collapse of the governments of Zelaya, Lugo, and Rousseff, together with the persistent legal persecution of Cristina Fernández de Kirchner and her top officials, have made it evident that what at the beginning of the century appeared as a punctual attack (limited to certain public figures and popular leaders) and which only violated or distorted some specific legal regulations, has now become a systematic attack on the Rule of Law. An attack, as shown in this remarkable book, to be waged at every opportunity on the political adversaries of Macrismo as the the constitutional edifice of Argentina crumbled piece by piece until its victims were not limited to the political opposition but now included all the inhabitants of this country. This work's detailed enumeration of this process jerks back the tattered curtain of justice, once embellished with virtuous republican symbols, and exhibits before the astonished eyes of the citizenship a group of people who, with refined perversity, have dedicated themselves to destroying one by one the pillars of due process in order to satisfy unspeakable designs and murky criminal interests.

As I went deeper into the endless labyrinth of legal malice, my astonishment at the perversity of its inspirers and executors constantly grew. Suddenly, as with my transformative visit to the Louvre, I began to see things I could not have imagined in even my most feverish hallucinations. I knew about the crisis of the rule of law in Argentina, and therefore about *lawfare*, but I never thought it could reach the extremes documented in this book. I was persuaded of the seriousness of the matter when, a few years ago, the editors-in-chief of two of Argentina's major newspapers, *Clarín* and *La Nación* (and behind them, the whole army of pseudo-journalists who poison our society from their radio and television shows) stepped up their attack on the lawfare concept. Elementary, my dear Watson: if they attack it must be real; if they say it does not exist, its existence must be overwhelmingly substantial. When they mocked those who appealed to that concept to describe the irritating vexations committed in the name of Justice, thus with capital letters, when they said that such a thing did not exist, that those who appealed to that word were accomplices of criminals who deserved to be in jail and that if they were already in jail it was because probing prosecutors and judges, with the law and the codes in hand, had determined their guilt beyond all reasonable doubt, when they argued with their sophistry, their falsehoods, and their sordid torrent of *fake news* against the existence of *lawfare*, I realized that the thing really did exist, that it was real, and that it deserved to be studied in detail. I did not have the opportunity to do so until I was able to read the book we are now discussing.

This book unravels this process of putrefaction that affects primarily, but not exclusively, the Federal Justice System. And it does so with sober and forceful arguments, because its vivid portrayal of both the nature and the number of violations to the Rule of Law saves thousands of words. The law has been disfigured to ensure the civil death of the enemies of the empire and of neoliberalism. If the military dictatorship made them physically disappear, now the officiants of *lawfare* make them legally disappear. Lula was not allowed to be a candidate for president in an election he would have easily won. Rafael Correa, probably the best president of Ecuador in more than a century and one of the most honest people I have ever met in my life, is banned from politics and serving an eight-year sentence for corruption. Evo Morales was also outlawed after his home was assaulted, looted and burned by the fascist hordes of Trump and Mike "Vito Genovese" Pompeo of Washington. Evo, accused of being a "terrorist!" In Paraguay, a legal clause drafted *ad hominen* prevents Fernando Lugo from being a candidate, and similar legal trickery also prevented Mel Zelaya from being a candidate in Honduras. In Argentina, the current vice-president Cristina Fernández de Kirchner has been harassed by an infinity of lawsuits whose sole purpose is to remove her definitively from the electoral field.[2]

Throughout the book, all of this is demonstrated with the cold precision of a surgeon. Its reading will captivate the reader, as it did me, because it is a true literary *thriller* that illustrates a new violation of the Rule of Law on every page. To begin with, the liquidation of the presumption of innocence, which

2   For a regional perspective on this legal pathology, see *Lawfare. Guerra judicial y neoliberal-ismo en América Latina*, a compilation by Silvina Romano with a foreword by Raúl Zaffaroni and the participation of Arantxa Tirado, Amilcar Salas Oroño, Camila Wollenweider, Javier Calderón Castillo, Bárbara Ester, Ava Gómez Daza and Giordana García Sojo, a publication of the Centro Estratégico Latinoamericano de Geopolítica, available at https://www. amazon .com/-/en/Silvina-M-Romano- ebook/dp/B082864MMV and where the situation of *lawfare* in different countries of the region is reviewed in detail.

forms the basis of modern criminal law and distinguishes it from the medie-val inquisition, which required the accused to prove his innocence and in the meantime sent him off to prison. We have returned to that barbaric law, as José Martí would say. It is appalling to learn that "in Argentina and throughout Latin America, pre-trial detention is used very, very much, even when there is no risk of flight or hindrance to the investigation."

Such a distortion of the judicial apparatus must have very deep-rooted causes. Why now? Because, as Raúl Zaffaroni writes in Chapter 1, "in recent decades, the supra-state power of financial capital has elevated the distribu-tive policy of states to the status of a *cosmic evil*, generating a veritable idola-try of the false market god." And "shameful criminal law" has as its mission to propitiate exemplary punishment for two categories of people: the poor, and the popular politicians. These are the targets of an endless flurry of attacks, in which the architects of "shameful criminal law," the media oligopolies and, in some cases, the legislators, also join forces. The media play the role of serial accusers and apply their enormous influence by manipulating public opinion with their huge and refined communications machinery, in which the tech-niques of fifth-generation warfare and *big data* combine to demonize popular figures who might embody an undesirable alternative to the forces of the *sta-tus quo*. Figures who are the diabolical embodiment of evil, of all that is wrong, of all the frustrations of what could have become a great nation and is not. Then, when the victim has already been subjected to a real media lynching and condemned by the public, now convinced that the politican in question is a Corrupt Person (a figure that, as this book makes clear, does not exist as such in the Penal Code), "Justice" makes its majestic entrance and issues the sen-tence that disqualifies or proscribes the popular leader. Clearly perceiving the psychological and psychosocial implications of this destruction of true justice, two scholars on the subject speak of the combination of *lawfare* and *lawfear*, that is, how the law, in its distortion and falsification, operates as an instrument to instill fear in the accused, their lawyers, the judges, the prosecutors them-selves (intimidated by corrupt colleagues), parapolice groups (as in Bolivia and Colombia), and the population in general.[3] Fear is instilled especially among public employees, second- or third-level officials, and social activists. The mes-sage is clear: "the reactivation of practices of fear, of persecution, in addition to media lynching" in order to persuade those who have the audacity to "get into politics" and seek to transform this world that they are entering a danger zone.

---

3   See *"Lawfare or Lawfear?* La guerra judicial y el miedo," by Silvina Romano and Camila Wollenweider, at https://www.celag.org/lawfare-o-lawfear-la-guerra-judicial-y-el-miedo/.

This reinforces, according to the authors, a kind of civil privatism, the individual correlate of the privatization of the State and the public, and vindicates anti-politics, the privatization of the individual, selfishness, and the rejection of collectivist strategies, all decisive components of the ideological conglomerate that neoliberalism needs to ensure its ongoing domination.

It is no coincidence that for at least forty years, ever since the Reagan Administration (1981–1989) and the "neoconservative revolution" that installed him in the White House, the United States has been engaged in the task of organizing and financing a series of advisory policies on legal issues and short courses on "best practices" in the fields of law, journalism, and legislation. It is not surprising, therefore, that recent research shows the crucial role played by Washington in promoting the judicial reforms adopted by numerous Latin American and Caribbean governments since the 1980s.[4] Such proposals were part of the package that came with the "conditionalities" demanded by the International Monetary Fund and the World Bank as part of the "structural adjustment" and stabilization policies of the neoliberal decade, and which were supposedly aimed at combating state corruption and inefficiency. As a result, the judicial apparatus (as well as the universities) were reorganized following the guidelines dictated by the White House, which created an impressive set of programs and institutions designed to implement these reforms. Some time later, the judiciary in our countries became, together with the oligopolized media system, a key player in delegitimizing governments, political parties and progressive leaderships. The "judicialization of politics" and its reverse, "the politicization, or partisanship, of justice" created the current black hole of *lawfare* that has been playing such a sinister role in recent times and of which this book gives a magnificent account. It should be noted that one of the most prominent participants in these "best practices" programs has been Judge Sergio Moro, the same judge who sentenced Lula to prison not based on evidence, of which he had none but because he had "intimate convictions" that Lula had committed a crime. In Argentina there are several judges and prosecutors who attended such courses and it is no coincidence that the current U.S. ambassador in our country since May 2018, Edward C. Prado, is a man with an extensive career in the field of U.S. justice, a former criminal court judge, and an active promoter of this type of training.[5]

---

4   See "Estados Unidos y la Asistencia Jurídica para América Latina y el Caribe" by Atilio Boron, Arantxa Tirado, Tamara Lajtman, Aníbal García Fernández and Silvina Romano and available at https://www.celag.org/eeuu-y-la-asistencia-juridica-para-america-latina/.

5   The ambassador has an exceptional resume in this field. According to the U.S. Embassy's website, he served as an appellate judge on the U.S. Court of Appeals for the Fifth Circuit, based in San Antonio, Texas. During his tenure, he was appointed by the Chief Justice of the U.S.

These "best practices" courses are intended to train those who would be in charge of removing undesirable politicians from the democratic game and of decreeing the political death of numerous popular leaders. Or, as evidenced in the notorious case of prosecutor Alberto Nisman, to redirect a fundamental investigation into a tragedy such as the AMIA bombing towards geopolitical interests favorable to the United States, even at the cost of sweeping away due process and of further delegitimizing the judicial system in the eyes of the public.[6] Courses, in short, where one learns how to demolish a rule of law that, with the passage of time, had begun to impede the smooth progress of global capitalism (and not only in Latin America and the Caribbean, but throughout the world). In the case of Bolivia, the destruction of the rule of law, as Zaffaroni rightly points out, has been total because the coup government of Jeanine Añez not only violates Bolivian norms and codes, but also disregards international law when, for example, the rights of asylum are not respected, or the guarantees that must be granted to the embassies of third countries are violated.

Supreme Court to chair the Criminal Court Review Committee, the Steering Committee of the Federal Judicial Center, the Defender Services Committee, and the judiciary Committee of the United States Judicial Conference. Prior to his tenure on the Fifth Circuit, Prado served for nineteen years as a district judge for the Western District of Texas. Before his judgeship, he served as a U.S. Attorney for the Western District of Texas. During his tenure as a federal prosecutor, he was appointed to the Attorney General's Advisory Commission. He also served as a state district judge, assistant federal public defender, and assistant district attorney in Texas. In the course of his duties, Prado also participated in multiple international judicial exchanges and academic meetings, programs and conferences on a variety of legal topics of importance to the strengthening of legal norms and systems throughout Latin America. Judge Prado visited Argentina and participated in programs focused on legal practice and common challenges facing both the United States and Argentina. In an interview shortly before arriving in Argentina he stated: "As a judge, I look forward to seeing how I can help the judicial branch. If there is an opportunity to put my experience to use, I am here to help. I am not here to tell you what you are going to do, but in my conversations with my judicial friends there are things we are working together on to improve Argentina's judicial system." *La Nación*, April 21, 2019. At https:// www.lanacion.com.ar/politica/edward-prado-el-nuevo -embajador-de-eeuu-en-el-pais-podemos-trabajar-juntos-untos-para-mejorar-el-sistema -judicial-argentino-nid2127770.

6   Regarding this case, quite illustrative of the machinations of lawfare, see Jorge Elbaum, *Efecto Nisman. Los usos políticos de una muerte* (Penguin Random House, Buenos Aires, 2019). In relation to the more generalized attack against those who oppose the dismantling of the Rule of Law see the complaint filed by the Argentine League for Human Rights before the United Nations Commission on Human Rights where it denounces "the alleged existence of a systematic and structural Plan of intimidation of the judiciary of the Argentine Republic." At https://spcommreports.ohchr.org/TmSearch/Results.

The chapter written by Cristina Caamaño is a detailed catalog of the multiple ways in which the fundamental principles of law have been undermined. There are so many transgressions and outrages in the cases she describes, that if one were also to take into account the abuses that take place in the many cases of people who are not public figures, or who are poor or homeless, the amount of violations of the law would be incalculable. The dubious methods used to achieve the destruction of justice are obvious, writes Caamaño, because the *modus operandi* is always the same, namely, to inundate the public with shocking headlines, always containing words with absolutely negative connotations. The most effective term is "corruption." The hegemonic media disseminates the news, she writes, regardless of whether or not it has any evidence to support it (that will have to be taken care of by the agents of the judiciary), while, attentive to the clamor of the "fourth branch" (the media), the judicial sector opens the case and begins to "collect the evidence." It does not matter if this consists of photocopies that cannot be examined, nor how the evidence was obtained, nor whether the constitutional guarantees of the accused have been respected. All that matters, Caamaño explains, is to "annihilate the political opponent" and condemn to political death those who oppose that sector that defends the most powerful economic groups. This may seem simplistic, but unfortunately it is not. It is the faithful and cruel reflection of the real destruction of the law. She neither deforms nor aggrandizes it. She simply describes it.[7]

Caamaño rightly insists, as does Zaffaroni, on the significance of violating the principle of fair trial. In this line, Vegh Weis's chapter provides an incredible piece of information when she refers to the consultation that Horacio Verbitsky made to Adrián Paenza, one of the most eminent Argentine mathematicians about the probability that "nine of the ten cases against former President Cristina Fernández would have fallen in only one of the twelve federal courts. Paenza calculated that with ten different cases and twelve possible courts, the chances that nine of the ten drawn at random would fall to only one of the courts – Claudio Bonadio's, as it happened – was 0.000000001777 percent. This miraculous result reflects the extremes to which the perversion and prostitution of Federal Justice in Argentina has reached.

In the third and final chapter of the work, Vegh Weis synthesizes the issue when she observes, on one of the first pages, that accusations of corruption are now the sword, and the courts the new battlefields. To elucidate the causes

---

7   See in this regard the dossier published by *Voces en el Fénix*, Publication of Plan Fenix, No. 63, July 2017 in which different facets of this problem are addressed.

and understand the scope of this situation – which lies at the foundation of *lawfare* – she appeals in the first place to the Freudian psychoanalytic tradition in order to help illuminate certain aspects of criminal law (transgression, guilt and punishment, for example), secondly to the sociological and political science perspective synthesized in the works of Pierre Bourdieu and Giovanni Sartori, which delve into the study of the media, especially television, and thirdly to studies on propaganda and the mass media. The conceptual framework she constructs is highly suggestive in that it creatively complements legal interpretations with the contributions and concrete findings of other theoretical traditions. This interdisciplinary perspective allows her, in my opinion, to "bring home" a coherent, highly persuasive explanation of a subject as delicate and socially significant as *lawfare*, a task that far exceeds the scope of judicial forums. But more than that, her articulation of these different approaches gives us a grim picture of the future of a society in which the techniques of propaganda and fifth-generation warfare have proven unprecedentedly effective in "formatting" the popular imagination. This situation, combined with a justice system at the service of the powers that be, increasingly concentrated and overbearing, has very harmful consequences for social life and the future of democracy. Indeed, it would be impossible to close our eyes to the challenges that the situation examined in this book presents for the future of democracy: the criminal confluence between corrupt (and corrupting) judges and prosecutors and the Goebbelsian media.

Some of the readers of this brilliant book may have encountered the phrase "economic hitman" (*sicariato económico*). There are also "media" and "judicial hitmen." Like a hired gun, the judicial hitman works on commission. Thanks to his position in the judiciary, this new type of killer can dispose of the life and property of his victims whenever he wishes, disregarding with total impunity not only the letter but also the spirit of the law, twisting fundamental legal premises (the presumption of innocence, fair trial, the right to defense, etc.), and incarcerating any whom the local ruling classes and their masters in the North consider enemies without any need for hard evidence. Like all hitmen, he works for pay, and he is rewarded magnificently for his despicable work. Judges and prosecutors enrich themselves obscenely or, like Sergio Moro in Brazil, receive a very special prize – in his case the appointment by Jair Bolsonaro to the post of Minister of Justice in recognition for the services he rendered by disqualifying Lula (though for some time now he has not been able to enjoy it).

This postface, which does not do full justice to the book, could hardly end without one final comment, not of a legal but of a theoretical nature, regarding the concept of democracy. It would come as no surprise to say that *lawfare* represents a mortal danger, and that fighting it is imperative, not only for those who want justice worthy of the name, but also for those who believe that democracy is an open-ended project that far exceeds the important, but insufficient, mechanics of electoral politics.[8] To make real a political regime that seriously intends to honor the great promise of democracy, that is, to achieve substantive and not only formal equality of citizens, to reverse neoliberalism's commodification of human rights (in healthcare, education, transportation, social security, etc.), to guarantee the responsible and revocable representation of elected officials, as well as an accountable and effective government of the majorities that protects the general welfare and happiness of the population, to do all of this, which is the core of a democratic agenda, we need true justice and not what, unfortunately, prevails today in Argentina and throughout Latin America. If there is no equality before the law – and it is precisely this premise that *lawfare* shuts down – there can be no equality in political life, and what we call democracy will become a spectral appearance behind which lurks a profoundly anti-democratic essence: the "legalized" tyranny of a minority articulated around financial capital, or, as they say today in the United States, the government of a rapacious plutocracy disguised in democratic garb. That is why we must thank Raúl Zaffaroni, Cristina Caamaño and Valeria Vegh Weis for their contributions to improve the quality of our democracies based on the implacable criticism of *lawfare*, its executors, and its inspirers.

---

8   We have examined this in depth in *Tras el búho de minerva, mercado contra democracia en el capitalismo de fin de siglo* (Fondo de Cultura Económica, Buenos Aires, 2000). More recently, on May 16, 2020, the subject was addressed by Rosana Actis in "Lawfare y Democracia," available at https://m.publico.es/columnas/110642923831/dominio-publico-lawfare-y-democra cia/amp.

Index

www.ingramcontent.com/pod-product-compliance
Lightning Source LLC
Chambersburg PA
CBHW062134040426
42335CB00039B/2161